CAREERING

CAREERING

Mike Piercy

Copyright © 2024 Mike Piercy

The moral right of the author has been asserted.

Apart from any fair dealing for the purposes of research or private study, or criticism or review, as permitted under the Copyright, Designs and Patents Act 1988, this publication may only be reproduced, stored or transmitted, in any form or by any means, with the prior permission in writing of the publishers, or in the case of reprographic reproduction in accordance with the terms of licences issued by the Copyright Licensing Agency. Enquiries concerning reproduction outside those terms should be sent to the publishers.

Troubador Publishing Ltd
Unit E2 Airfield Business Park
Harrison Road, Market Harborough
Leicestershire LE16 7UL
Tel: 0116 279 2299
Email: books@troubador.co.uk
Web: www.troubador.co.uk

ISBN 978 1 80514 480 9

British Library Cataloguing in Publication Data.
A catalogue record for this book is available from the British Library.

Printed and bound by CPI Group (UK) Ltd, Croydon, CR0 4YY
Typeset in 11pt Minion Pro by Troubador Publishing Ltd, Leicester, UK

SINCERE THANKS

To the thousands of children who have inspired – and to their parents for forbearance.

To Jonathan Smith for advice, encouragement and writing '*The Learning Game*', a well-thumbed copy of which should be on every teacher's bookshelf.

To Frankie, Ed, Charlie and Anna for being wonderful people.

To Lucy, for love and support.

CONTENTS

Preface	ix
Beginnings	1
Lessons in Leadership	24
Senior Management	32
Headship	43
Faith	57
A Fresh Start	70
A Move to Sevenoaks	87
Parents & Partnership	97
Hierarchy	113
Mission	122
Frankie	137
Leadership Style	144
Storm Clouds	155
2020: Covid-19	159
France	177
Tonbridge School	184
Knowing the Time is Right	202
In Conclusion	214
Bibliography and References	225

PREFACE

0700 hours, already at the desk, preparing; planning for another busy day. The school is eerily quiet, in darkness, as yet untrodden – in stark contrast to the daytime bustle and noise. The top bunk boarders on the floor above, my alarm clock as they land heavily on the floor, the ceiling cracked and shaking. The concentrated silence is shattered by the doorbell. At this time of day?

Through the glass, backlit, I spy a nemesis. His evident agitation is felt even through a locked door. He is admitted, welcomed with an innocent, cheery greeting, which is immediately dismissed, the white froth of spittle already forming in the corners of his mouth.

'I warned you!' The first words, spat rather than spoken, are followed by the demand for an immediate meeting with me and the Deputy Head. I proceed to a distant office to collect her, the furious, quivering man left seething in the hallway. We return to be subjected to a forty-five minute tirade of threats and verbal abuse, the opportunity for response or rebuttal rebuffed. And then he storms away leaving a crackling aura so palpable it stings the eyes. Ten minutes later, the morning staff briefing has to be conducted with customary calm. A life in the day of a Head.

How many of us have a clearly defined career plan from age eighteen? Few, I would suggest. The twenty-first century world, the fourth industrial revolution, technology and artificial intelligence dictate more frequent career changes over the course of a working life. A recent phenomenon, anomalous to me, is those in the infancy of their working lives becoming 'consultants'. This, we thought, was the province of those who have worked through a long career, changing jobs, gathering experience with maturity then, and only then, moving to advisory roles for organisations using their sphere of expertise.

For many today, therefore, and probably for most in years gone by, we career from situation to situation, from job to job, until a coherent plan emerges or serendipity takes us where it will. Roald Dahl prefaces his book *Boy* by saying it is not an autobiography; yet of course it is the tale of his schooling and life – albeit an intermittent story of those events that have stayed with him.

Neither is this an autobiography. It is an account of how early years in Africa, education, schooling and experience led me to career up the ladder to Headship of three very different schools. It will give an insight to the British Prep School world and its eccentricities. The treasured independence of these schools, their freedom from the homogeneity of education, their sometimes arcane traditions, allow children to develop their uniqueness, their individuality – even idiosyncrasy.

Some of the content will be glaringly obvious to those in the wonderful teaching profession. I hope other parts might affirm, reassure and encourage. As for parents, the inside knowledge, an educator's experience and views, might inform and entertain.

BEGINNINGS

Laurie Lee was 'set down' from the carrier's cart in rural Gloucestershire. I was set down from a BOAC VC10; met at Heathrow from Lagos, Nigeria, by a stranger from The British Wives' Society. 2024 Google finds no trace of this organisation, which helped with the children of expatriate families in transit to their boarding schools – a reflection of changed times where 'guardians' are heavily vetted and regulated.

Lagos at the time, 1966, was an unsettled place, mid-Biafran war with a subsequent series of violent coups d'état. Sending expatriate children back to a UK boarding school for their education – in the many senses of the word – was an obvious choice. For us as children, when in Lagos, it was an exciting and idyllic life with a seemingly endless succession of parties and social events within the generally British expatriate community. We were less conscious of the dangers and threats our parents must have felt. My brother and I were rudely woken one night by a tremendous noise, bringing our mother to our room and our father following, giving rather impatient reassurance, his sleep disturbed, that it was just a thunderstorm. The next morning the truth was revealed: a nearby petrol station had been bombed. We were living in a war zone. While much of the conflict was in the south-east of the country, Lagos was far from immune.

We were in Nigeria because my father worked for a bank which dictated that any children could be educated at a boarding school in the UK – a bane and a boon for all concerned. Prior to that, primary education was at St. Saviour's School, Ikoyi, Lagos, its website suggesting the school thrives today. Of these early educational days there is minimal recollection other than single storey buildings, sparse grass and a dusty playground. My mother spoke many years later of a rare intervention when told the teacher had been enforcing right-handed writing on a very obvious left-hander.

Holding a very senior position in the bank, my father sometimes had to inspect branches in other parts of the country. One memorable school holiday, a light aircraft and pilot were chartered to visit remote places – the roads dangerous, often incomplete – and the family was to travel with him on this occasion. Nigeria has tremendous geographical, cultural and linguistic variety. It was a country rent asunder by internecine rivalry. We avoided the oil-rich south-east, the home of the Igbo and the heart of the conflict against the mainly south-western, ruling Yoruba who were central to government and allegedly squandering the oil wealth, to the huge resentment of the Igbo. Our colonial past has left deep and artificial divisions across Africa. We travelled north to Ibadan, Jos and Kano flying for many hours over deep, impenetrable jungle with no onboard loo and nowhere to land if a youthful bladder had the calling, as I vividly and painfully recall.

Our back gate opened onto the sixteenth tee of the Ikoyi Golf Club, where we were members and frequent players with our caddies, who were also very good coaches, chipping onto browns – oiled sand. Back then there was no irrigation to sustain greens. In the heat and humidity of the early afternoon when the course was deserted my brother and I would wander out in search of lost golf balls, wary of snakes and scorpions. One Sunday afternoon we took a family walk over the course on the far side of which bordered the main, military Dodan Barracks. We were sent packing with forceful shouted warnings and not just guns but heavy artillery, an anti-aircraft gun pointed in our direction.

The Ikoyi Club itself, golf, swimming, social, was a hub for friends and was where my father used to get a haircut. He joked when comparing his 'five-bob barber' in the gents' loo relative to colleagues' expensive haircuts in their London clubs. There was a children's cocktail, a 'Chapman', which mixed Fanta Orange and Sprite with a little Angostura bitters over ice made with filtered water. Age alters spatial awareness and perspective; the pool seemed enormous with lofty, death-defying diving-boards.

Television was black and white, the bulk of programmes Nigerian-produced, like *The Bar Beach Show*, where I remember a hat gently floating down from above the staging onto the grand piano, those offstage occasionally accidentally wandering into the live broadcast. *Colombo*, with the wonderful Peter Falk, is the only imported programme I recall. As to other entertainment, there were films sent out from the UK; big reels and a 16mm projector shining the moving images onto white, external walls. One Christmas we (or neighbours) had sent for *Gunfight at the O.K. Corral*. Duly, surprisingly delivered on time, watched in silent, awed excitement, the last reel was missing. No gunfight.

Victoria Island was a destination for families at weekends. At the time sparsely populated and underdeveloped, I understand it is now another thriving, packed suburb of Lagos. It was also the location for government or military executions. I seem to remember these were carried out weekly, on a beach, open to a public audience, well attended and I think, incredibly, sometimes televised.

We would be driven to The Federal Palace Hotel on Victoria Island, taking a boat to Takwa Bay where the bank had a beach chalet for employees and their families. On one side was a protected lagoon for swimming and, on the other, the more violent waves of the Gulf of Guinea. Any travel in the city could be treacherous; Lagos always seemed militarised with frequent army checkpoints. On one trip to Victoria Island we were summarily stopped at an army checkpoint. The soldiers seemed unusually agitated and, as a consequence, my parents more than a little anxious. Sitting in the back I wound down the window and innocently asked to see the soldier's gun. Nigerians adore children – even expatriate ones. My request was disarming for he showed me the gun with pleasure, with evident pride, then waved us through.

Ikoyi was – and still is, I understand – one of, if not the, residential area of choice in Lagos. Large compounds, houses, many with swimming pools, all with security guards and house staff. We had an enclosed, covered back yard which, as Christmas approached, housed the live, gobbling turkeys and a goat, which were generously given every year, all of which were donated to the house staff who lived in a separate building adjacent to our house. My father had a chauffeur who took him to and from his offices on The Marina, central Lagos, the subject of his ire when, somehow, he broke the gear change mounted on the Citroen steering column.

We had security guards in the grounds day and night. The nightwatch carried a bow and arrow, which, to my brother and me, was terribly exciting. Underlying, however, was the threat to security in an unstable city, which our parents must have felt much more keenly. Although we were both at school in England I do remember my mother telling us of an occasion when burglars broke into the house. My father woke to a shadowy figure moving beside his bed. He jumped up, stark naked, and courageously, perhaps rashly, chased the man from the house. The means of entrance was discovered to be a relatively small broken window on which one of the intruders had gashed himself, leaving a lengthy, bloody trail across the cream carpet. The nightwatch was found to be comatose with suspected substances – self or otherwise administered – having rendered him so.

Careering

How many parents advise their children to follow their own career choices? I would advocate quite the opposite, fingers burnt by their own experiences. My father, a remote, somewhat distant figure at the best of times, was clear in advising against banking despite being very successful himself, having risen from Merseyside branch teller to Managing Director, Nigeria. He entertained John Major, who worked for the same bank at that time. My mother would host huge business dinner parties, on one occasion the Nigerian Chairman coming for lunch in his beautifully tailored Savile Row suit and sockless Cheaney shoes. With the privilege of having attended a prestigious 'public' school, my father might have hoped for prime ministerial (or what some may see as more lofty) aspirations and not teaching, but there it was – the calling which came for me in time and quite by accident.

Two school holidays a year were spent in Lagos with our parents taking their annual leave in England, usually over Easter. The trips to Heathrow and flights back home were always febrile with excitement in anticipation of being home, seeing our parents and enjoying the privileged expatriate lifestyle. In a rare adolescent gesture of consideration for my mother, who loved apples and was deprived of them in Lagos, I once bought a bag to take onto the plane and hand to her on arrival. The man at immigration and customs was clearly oblivious to the kindness, emphatically declaring they were not permitted, smashing them on the table with his bare fist. Lagos' Ikeja airport was a place to be negotiated with caution and the bank employed someone to grease the wheels of security, accelerating and easing us through the airport.

Those who went to boarding school in the '70s will have countless tales, many of which may well be shocking to any audience, never mind one of the 2020s. I will not dwell; it was a different age, though a few shared anecdotes give an impression.

At Prep School the Head or Housemaster has huge influence. In my case it was one and the same person, Head and Housemaster, a bachelor graced with neither warmth nor kindness. In his defence, however, I may not have been the easiest of charges. For an expatriate child this figure is central to wellbeing. As for the parents, their child is entrusted to him in every aspect of care. He was also the Latin teacher, reclining in his chair on a dais, finger dabbling with nostrils, rolling and flicking, declining *mensa*, which we repeated parrot fashion – or *bellum*: 'bla, bla'. Eyes rarely left the clock carelessly located above his head, next to which was a poster bearing big, bold letters: *Tempus Fugit*. Not in his lessons.

At this tender age I developed a love of music. I learnt the piano. My teacher's claim to fame was her hands being those on a keyboard which featured in the 1971 film *The Go-Between*. She would munch biscuits quietly in the corner, farting in what she believed to be a discreet manner, while I fumbled my way through scales and arpeggios. It was a small room. I took up the double bass with an instrument that had to be re-strung for a left-hander, later playing Saint Saëns' *The Elephant* in school concerts. Class music was taught by a delightful man. He was, however, afflicted with a short temper, easily aroused by disruptive non-musical pupils. Board rubbers flew. They were very different times.

Aged nine I was unwell – increasingly so. The symptoms exhibited were stomach pains, vomiting, keeping nothing down, along with a developing fever – none of which was abating. It does not take a qualified medical practitioner to recognise these as classic symptoms of appendicitis, yet the Head made me get up and attend school, ignoring the matron's protestations. Eventually she prevailed or, quite possibly, made her own decision, overruling the Head. I was taken to 'The San' at the Senior School where the nurse immediately called the doctor, who quickly phoned for an ambulance and I was rushed to the Jenny Lind Children's Hospital in Norwich. I vividly recall the uncomfortable, bumpy ride through the bends of North Norfolk's winding roads, siren sounding, blue light flashing. Surgery that afternoon was emergency: the appendix had ruptured and peritonitis a life-threatening risk. Two weeks in hospital followed with a foul drain protruding from the wound.

My mother had been due to fly back to the UK for the Easter holidays and, through emergency, brought the date forward. On release from hospital, my recovery continued in our home at that time in nearby Aylsham. I recall my mother saying she had been to see the Head, who I expect had been shown no mercy. My return to school in the autumn was tinged with awkwardness.

I attended Gresham's School in beautiful Holt. My parents chose it because they wished to retire to North Norfolk, and because expatriate friends had chosen the school and were happy with it. Senior School choice today is a far more complex, convoluted process. Old School House (now no more) was in the centre of Holt, some three quarters of a mile from the main school, which I think made us all seem rather different from the outset – outliers. I was fortunate in having an older brother for support, which was of immeasurable value. It was otherwise, however, a lonely existence – far from the outstanding pastoral care I now see in boarding schools. One miserable Sunday I made a reverse charge call to Lagos on the house payphone, begging to be taken away. It must have been deeply upsetting for my parents, many thousands of miles apart through a crackly phone line.

For their time in the UK and in anticipation of retirement they later found a beautiful house just outside Wymondham, south-west of Norwich, making it into a lovely, rural home and garden. The quaint address placed it in 'Rightup Lane'. Norfolkish is an indigenous language: Wymondham pronounced 'Windham'; Stiffkey pronounced 'Stookey'. My mother was baffled when refurbishing the house and the builder referring to a shop in Norwich selling 'pearly carpets' – translated to 'purely'. A delightful sign remains today just outside Wiveton, near the coast: 'Slow you down.' The bulk of the garden was an expansive, bowling green lawn which was terrorised by moles. Strangely they would disappear for a few months, like clockwork, at the same time each year. When asked why or where they went, our gardener would reply emphatically, with absolute conviction, 'Thetford!', some twenty miles distant.

Many of my teachers have blended into a greyness. Most memorable was my maths teacher who somehow got me through A Level. He kept two large Alsatian dogs barricaded behind his desk and, when coming to give individual help at my desk after a morning break, would say, sotto voce, 'Still on the Woodbines, Piercy?'

A new, young, dynamic, approachable teacher, who can be known as Dr. B, made an impression. A few of us got into a chatty, friendly, informal conversation with him and, either deliberately or carelessly, we sauntered onto the subject of his responsibility as a member of staff in upholding the school rules. We posed the theoretical question of his actions if he found pupils in a pub and were delighted with his answer: if the pupils ignored him, he would do likewise. We felt this to be incredibly enlightened.

Saturdays were busy with morning lessons and afternoon sport. Sunday morning was chapel followed by lunch in the blandly named 'Central Feeding Block', after which was the prospect of some freedom. Living at school and in a boarding house away from the main campus, we all had bikes and Sunday afternoons often saw a ride to the coast: Blakeney, Salthouse or Weybourne. This particular Sunday four of us, aged seventeen, decided our best plan was to visit The King's Head pub in Letheringsett – that of *Lord Cozens Hardy* by John Betjeman – en route to the coast. Having ordered our four pints, the barman placed the brimming glasses and I paid. It was only then I looked across and saw, in the corner, Dr. B. The lurch of the stomach when caught out will be familiar to all.

Remembering our recent, informal conversation, we took our glasses into the garden, drank quickly and pedalled away.

Monday morning assembly in Big School. The Head, Logie Bruce-Lockhart, began to round things off with notices for the week, culminating in the order that I and my three friends should report to his study at break. 'The Doosh', as he was known ('*Il Duce*'), was a fair, decent and honourable man but we knew what fate would befall us: the option of the cane or 'gating'. Thus was the custom in those days. It may seem somewhat counter-intuitive but caning was normally chosen over gating. To be gated was to be confined to barracks, the deprivation of freedom for some weeks, which was deeply unappealing in a full boarding school; no weekend cycle rides or visits to the town of a Wednesday or Saturday afternoon. He asked what we had done the previous day and, knowing he knew, we confessed. Four strokes of the cane followed. There was nothing cruel or spiteful in his actions; it's just the way things used to be.

I did later have a conversation with Dr. B about the matter, reminding him of our previous conversation and sensing a smidge of embarrassment. Children are quick to judge and quicker to spot unfairness. Inconsistency is looked upon unfavourably, to the detriment and diminution of respect for the teacher, something which remained with me throughout my teaching career and, later, Headship.

My recollection of careers advice was something called the 'ISCO Test', which categorises jobs into groups, looking at the traits, characteristics and interests submitted by the individual then arriving at career suggestions. I seem to recall my top recommendation was to work in a supermarket. The only career ambition I did have was to join the navy, for its own intrinsic sake, the appeal of travel and the perceived glamour – admittedly a rather naïve, youthful, romantic vision. A friend had a navy scholarship and would be going to Dartmouth Royal Naval College. My father had served in the navy in the Second World War and had told some wonderful stories, no doubt with more than a little embellishment.

With hindsight, I was deluded. It would have been entirely the wrong career: too structured; too controlled. As it happened I had been diagnosed with short sight when about ten and wore glasses, thereby ruling out a position as deck officer. How had I survived so long in a classroom with a blackboard and preferred location as far from the teacher as possible? With barely a scientific cell in my body, I was never going to pursue the more technical side. The navy was not an option.

I meandered my way through what was undoubtedly a generally good, privileged education with some fine teaching but, without an emotional keel, rudder or career-defining compass, I emerged with poor results. A friend was going into the city to join a stock-broking firm and suggested I do the same. Another friend was taking a gap year to work in a Prep School and this seemed like a good interim plan, which I copied. Applying to Gabbitas, Truman & Thring, they came up with a number of offers. More recently, for understandable reasons of perception, rebranded 'Gabbitas', this was not an extract from the staff list at Hogwarts but an organisation which advised and recruited for the independent sector of education and continues to do so. I did not just one but two years as a gap student and had stumbled upon my career choice by accident before heading into tertiary education and a degree.

The gap years were spent at a proprietary (privately owned) school in Weymouth, Dorset – now no more. The Head was the owner, with his ancient, formidable mother resident in the main building. When summoned to her grand apartment, staff prepared as if for an audience with the Queen. When the boarders made too much noise in the evening, she would emerge with unconcealed fury and woe betide anyone in her path – boys or staff. Very young, fresh out of school – bearded to disguise my youthful face when supervising boys only two years younger – the staff were kind and supportive. A mere boy, I was thrown in amongst some very experienced teachers who were warm and welcoming. I was, unknowingly, learning much about what was to become my trade.

A green eighteen, I was assigned to classes of pupils aged up to sixteen. Heaven knows what I taught, and indeed what they learnt, but it was 'in-service' training at the sharp end that would reap later benefits. I do recall reading Thor Heyerdahl's book *The Kon-Tiki Expedition* with one class. A boy, reading aloud, misread the word 'tentacles': 'the octopus has a large beak between its testicles.' Of course, the class fell about into paroxysms of laughter – me included. Whether he was playing up this young master or not, it was a shared moment between class and teacher, a bonding which enhances mutual respect and thus learning in any classroom. To reprimand would have been wrong.

Retrospectively, I think one reason why I stayed the two years was because my father, after a short illness and rapid decline, died aged a mere fifty-seven years. Having gone to boarding school aged eight, I was only beginning to get to know my own father when he was tragically plucked away. His was a long, successful career reaching very dizzy heights then taking an early, well-deserved retirement to Norfolk. My mother had lost her husband less than two years later. I passed my driving test and bought a beaten-up Austin Allegro (a misnomer if there ever was one) that enabled me to get to Norfolk in school holidays and half terms to support my bereaved mother. An early lesson in car management was learnt when I left the handbrake off to find the car parked in the school science lab one morning. The second year in Weymouth and the passing of time galvanised me to do something a little more academic; to strive for a degree and pursue a career in teaching.

The World of Work

Somehow attaining a third-class degree – I was still a poor student – my first post-graduate job was once again at a proprietary Prep School: West Downs in Winchester. The owner, Jerry Cornes, was a charismatic, even legendary, figure, having been a middle-distance runner in the 1932 and 1936 Olympics. The man I encountered and who employed me in 1985 was still a hugely impressive figure although whisky and Silk Cut had begun to take their toll. He and his wife, Rachael (Ray), were the proprietors with the Headship delegated to Reg Severn. Though young and naïve as I must have been, it was not difficult to tell the relationship was strained.

Jerry Cornes bought West Downs in 1953. It was already a traditional Prep School (at the time just for boys) serving Senior Schools such as Eton and Winchester. There seemed to be something of a fashion in the first half of the twentieth century of establishing or buying a Prep School. The proprietor, usually also the Head, was often an autocratic character whose homemade rules withstood all interference. The proprietor having delegated leadership to another, yet remaining in the building, was unlikely to create a harmonious relationship.

A charming, eccentric figure, larger than life, Jerry was clearly devoted to the school. There was a balcony facing the road where he once appeared, crying out, 'Help, why won't someone help?' or words to that effect. Passers-by gathering on the pavement beyond may well have thought he was about to hurl himself over the balustrade, but no, he was calling to maintenance staff to help him move furniture and beds before the start of term. As an aside, the balcony on which he stood, neglected by maintenance and budget, looked distinctly perilous.

I was a 'Junior Master' teaching general subjects – I recall history, maths and English, with sport a prerequisite for many staff as per the Prep School way. The imposing building started life in the late nineteenth century, purpose built as Winchester Modern School – a magnificent, gothic, brick and flint edifice facing Romsey Road leading into the city, conveniently (for a boarding Prep School) close to Winchester prison, the hospital and King Alfred's teacher training college, which today, ironically, occupies the property.

Much of the length of the ground and first floors was classrooms, some divided by moveable partitions. A disadvantage to this was the heating pipes which ran beneath and along the length of the classrooms, for a dead mouse, taking its last breath, would cleave to the pipes for warmth, thereby gracing all classrooms with its terminal waft. Dormitories were on the second floor with one girls' dormitory curiously and carelessly named 'Continent'. The simple question 'Which dormitory are you in?' had a regrettable response.

There was an unusual educational structure in that pupils (co-ed by the time I joined) could be promoted – or demoted – from a class or set on a termly basis, hence moving down the corridor via those partitions. Classes were small. There seemed to be no stigma about this; it was just taken as the way things were done. The moves must have been based on conceptual development rather than curriculum content with the aim of successfully achieving places at highly selective Senior Schools.

In schools and education as a whole, there is a danger of systems existing for the sake of the system and conformity, the same for all, rather than for the benefit of each individual child. What may seem radical in one context can be exactly right in another. Why not accelerate or hold back a child in a group that differs from chronological age if it enhances learning and personal development? Many years later I would use the expression, 'You cannot accelerate conceptual development,' in response to the temptation of tutoring.

Another oddity of West Downs (even then and certainly now) was the arrangements for staff. Male staff inhabited 'The Masters' Lodge' – a separate building – while the female staff occupied 'The Ladies' Sitting Room' in the main building. For those staff who were resident, dinner was taken every weekday evening in The Masters' Lodge and 'the ladies' were meant to knock before entering. This a mere thirty-eight years ago.

The Masters' Lodge had other benefits such as a long first-floor corridor which made a perfect indoor cricket net with polished boards on which the bowler – keeping the flight low – could even make a tennis ball turn. It also housed an eclectic group of colleagues who influenced and sometimes inspired this absolute novice. One had previously run his own business and, being of mathematical disposition, had turned to teaching on selling up to a bigger competitor. Another, lecturing those training as teachers at nearby King Alfred's College, taught maths to those taking academic scholarships. His gravitas and experience placed him at the head of the table. For schools such as Eton and Winchester, the curriculum encroached on elements of the A Level syllabus. Maths, then and now, needs to be taught by someone with a mathematically wired brain, which both of these men had, albeit from very different backgrounds.

It was a somewhat eccentric common room. I recall one instance where another young master had damaged the ligaments in his ankle but carried on with his teaching and duties with the help of crutches. There was a rule of no running in the long classroom corridor – narrow and with polished wooden flooring. To do so was hazardous. This gentleman was standing in the corridor chatting to the French teacher when a boy came hurtling along. He raised his crutch as a barrier, telling the boy to walk. The child, halted in his tracks, apologised, moving on at a safer pace. The French teacher, of French birth and parentage, still acquiring the vagaries of the English language, turned to the colleague, saying with some admiration and in all apparent innocence, 'You have a magnificent weapon in your crutch.'

The greatest influence on my early development as a teacher was a chap whom we'll call J; he would be embarrassed by what follows if he were to be named. He ran the 1st XI and could not only successfully execute bicycle kicks, he would also put the ball in the net with the same gymnastic move. The boys were in awe. Here was my first true mentor. J was Head of English; with a passion for literature and language, he imparted his enthusiasm to his charges with some panache. He had a teaching style which was firm with high expectations of his pupils yet with a lightness of touch. Humour was never far away and in achieving this delicate balance, the pupils held him in high regard. His results at Common Entrance and in Scholarship exams were amongst the best in the school. J's role as 1st XI coach also put him on something of a pedestal – for the boys in particular. West Downs was not a big school and yet it very much punched above its weight on the football field and cricket pitch, never mind having an impressive academic success rate, with many pupils proceeding to highly selective Senior Schools.

Early in my career I became the organiser of school ski trips. Aged just twenty-five I was in charge of a group of children travelling to Austria – something that would never be allowed today and quite rightly so. The brash confidence of youth: I was not truly conscious of the huge responsibility. I was also a novice skier and only began to master the technique by carrying a large box which had contained the pupils' packed lunches; box in both hands, poles dangling, skiing back down the mountain. Getting the balance wrong, not facing down the mountain, would have sent me slithering, crashing, no doubt to the merriment of assembled pupils, not a vestige of dignity remaining.

One day at the lunchtime meeting point, at the designated time after their lesson, two pupils were missing. It was thought they might have been playing in the snow to the side of the slope just below where we were. I left the group to go in search and, not finding them, got on the chairlift to rejoin the group. At this point it started snowing. And then the chairlift stopped. I was stranded mid-air, swaying in the breeze, a layer of snow beginning to cover me, getting very chilly. It seemed an eternity, fear in the pit of my stomach, hanging there for some twenty minutes before the chair began moving again – anxiety about the missing children growing by the moment, with no mobile phones in those days. I skied back over to the group to find the missing two had returned almost immediately after I had left. School ski trips, often with entire families joining us, became very much part of my life – at whichever school. I even spent the turn of the century with a group of about eighty children, parents and even grandparents in beautiful Kitzbühel, Austria.

Later in my career and especially as Head I became very cautious of socialising with parents – mixing business with pleasure. In one school, at a parents' ball I was standing by the bar when a parent approached asking if I knew the whereabouts of her child's missing sweater. Many years on, through the school of one of our children, we made a rare exception of going to dinner with one family to find a gathering of at least ten school families. We were the first to leave due to babysitter limitations and learnt afterwards from a reliable source that car keys found their way to the middle of the table later in the evening. The next week the hosts' son was in trouble at school. The parents descended on me with fury in complete denial of his wrongdoing, all thoughts of notional friendship banished.

Such was not the case in the 1980s. Perhaps it was the ethos of West Downs. It was arguably a different, less oppositional era. Later learning the responsibility of Headship where everything comes back to your desk was definitely a factor. I recall lengthy Sunday lunches, wine flowing, with one delightful family who had a son and daughter at the school. They became firm friends. West Downs was a cricketing school with a strong parental following. For the longer matches on home ground – a magnificent cricket square – families would set up for the day with their picnics, wine, champagne and the early days of Australian lager imported to Britain. There were parent weekend barbecues to which staff were openly invited and most welcome with tremendous hospitality. I remember one where the host offered a coffee as we left, insisting it should be laced with Calvados. In fact, it was Calvados laced with coffee, a liquor I avoided for many years after.

Jerry's office was a dusty garret on the second floor, paper-strewn and book-strewn, with an aura of stale tobacco. I was summoned one morning, shocked to hear the first words without any courteous preamble: 'Mike, I'm afraid you'll have to go.' At twenty-five years old and learning, enjoying the school, teaching and colleagues, it was an utterly devastating sentence. He continued, 'Pupil numbers aren't strong and we have to make savings.' It was a case of 'last in, first out'. I was to be best man for J that summer and was then out of the door. No doubt employment law in 1987 gave the employee rights, and today, employment can be terminated within the first two years of contract but with the complementary factor of pay in lieu of notice. None of that applied – I had to seek another position with no recompense.

A job as English teacher was advertised in a Prep School attached to a Senior School. The influence of J had been considerable and English was to become my chosen subject. I applied and was successful with a prerequisite move to another part of the country.

One thing can be said of an expatriate upbringing and, possibly, boarding school: either or both make it easier to face change and adapt. At this formative stage of my adulthood, I did not aspire to Headship, any management position or indeed teaching as a lifetime profession. There was no clear path; I was still careering, with fortune – or some might say misfortune – my guiding light. I was cutting my teaching teeth, observing and learning from those around me – for better or for worse.

There is a paradox in my own school experiences. I bore Logie Bruce-Lockhart no ill will for the caning – and it happened more than one once as I had joined the smoking crowd at school. Every action has a consequence and we knew what that would be. He was honest, fair and consistent. Talking to pupils later in my career, regaling tales of caning, their eyes widen and their mouths open in shock. In the pupils' eyes at least, the Head is held up as a paragon of virtue, on a moral pedestal, guilty of no sin. Then I recall the duplicitous Dr. B, who put a deep dent in my trust of teachers. In contrast there was the Housemaster of the newly opened girls' house, who happened to be in the room of the girl I was calling to from outside and who simply said, 'Michael Piercy, go away!' I did – with a smile and deeper respect. I believe such recollections from my own school days have reinforced an empathy, an affinity, with those who find school and academic learning not to be their natural habitat.

These stories, those which precede and which follow, may give a misleading, unintentional impression of those early days when fortune was unkind and I was hard done by, the world of work being a cruel, unkind place – neither the intention nor indeed the reality. The very fact

I recall certain incidents so many years later indicates the profound and lasting impression they made, which may have had an influence – conscious or otherwise – on my choices and practice when rising eventually to leadership.

LESSONS IN LEADERSHIP

The summer of 1987 was spent moving from Hampshire to the home counties – encumbered by few possessions in those days having hitherto lived in school accommodation. I settled into a school flat, sharing with another young teacher whose cigarette smoke infused the small flat only moments after his morning alarm sounded. A resolute character, he decided one day to quit and did – that was it. Amongst him and others, I was again fortunate to work with a fine team of colleagues, learning from them all what was becoming my profession. The neighbouring classroom was occupied by a Northern Irishman who taught French. We would meet in the corridor between lessons, trying to speak French with a Welsh accent – much to the amusement of passing pupils.

Reaching my late twenties, friends were quicker than me to embrace marriage and I was excited to be invited to a wedding in St. Andrew's, Scotland. The wedding day would be preceded by a round of golf on that very famous course, meaning I would have to leave work on the

Thursday evening at the very latest. I sought permission, which was not granted – of course deeply disappointing and, with hindsight, surprising. Even then, in the embryo years of a career, and more so in later years, I realised that working in a boarding school requires dedication and complete commitment during term-time. When such special opportunities arise, permitting absence for a colleague will earn far more loyalty and commitment than disruption in short-term cover needed for absence. Above all, it is just the right thing to do.

Walking into the common room one break time, I knew there was mischief afoot with a subdued air, febrile with anticipation. How very different things were in the late 1980s: no emails, no mobiles, no text messaging. Internal communication was via meetings, minutes, letters and noticeboards. Most staff common rooms would have a Head's noticeboard, a staff board and a felt board with criss-cross ribbon, into which could be slipped a more urgent note – rather than using the eponymous pigeonhole. I remember with amusement that the Deputy Head used to remind us the pigeonhole was for regular attention and not a filing system.

Most staff would check that felt board on entering the common room, the Head being no exception, one day seeing a brown envelope bearing his name. He opened it and out tumbled a collection of advertisements for science teachers (he was a science teacher by training) cut out from the *Times Educational Supplement*. There was a heavy silence, over which, after a pause, he muttered, 'I don't think I'm very popular at the moment,' and left the room. It was a shocking, unkind trick but the force of a common room was very evident.

During my first year I was asked to be a boarding house tutor, agreeing with some reluctance as I was enjoying the freedom of being non-resident. The Head said it would only be for a year, after which I would be made a Head of Day House, of which there were several. I acquiesced – hopefully with good grace. Come the end of that boarding year, back to the Head's common room board, there was posted a note announcing the appointment of a colleague to the day house. In a private meeting I sought soon after, I reminded the Head of his promise. To no avail. The appointment had been made and announced. Summoned to meet the Senior School Head, I explained the situation, feeling the essential bond of trust between Head and teacher had been broken. Beyond repair. I reverted to the *Times Educational Supplement* and began looking for yet another job.

Seeking a position in the middle of the summer term was going to be a challenge. After two rather short-term positions with very mixed experiences, fortune was kind. Great Ballard, a small Prep School nestling in the South Downs near Chichester, was seeking a Head of English; an unanticipated step, or indeed leap, careering up the ladder. A slight reservation was the prospect of another proprietary school. The newly appointed young Head, however, was dynamic and ambitious for his school and we got on well at interview. Grasping the opportunity when the job was offered, I was to be Head of English and, with some irony, resident House Tutor.

The building which housed Great Ballard, originally Regency and remodelled by Lutyens, approached via a short drive, was captivating, as were the grounds and South Downs around. Just outside the gates in the hamlet of Eartham was The George Inn – undeniably of further appeal. Classrooms were alongside the imposing main house in a series of buildings, at the centre of which was a hall – or gym – with science labs and a Pre-Prep adjacent in what had once been a walled garden. Playing fields were across the road, with the ground rising steeply behind the Lutyens house to woodland and, at the top, views of the coast. It was a stunning setting. Get prospective parents down the drive and they would be sold.

A great boarding Prep School tradition is fireworks night, which brings the pupil, parent and staff community together. Great Ballard was no exception. Generally speaking, every common room has a pyromaniac who is excited to light the fuse – though not always entirely compliant with health and safety requirements.

Predating my time at Great Ballard there was a great story of the previous, proprietary Head who was so inclined. The rising hill to the back of the school was called 'The Mound', making the perfect arena for such a display with spectators at the bottom on the lawn and the younger, more cautious ones in the dormitories on the first floor watching through expansive, wide open sash windows. The pyromaniac's mistake was to store the fireworks in an uncovered wheelbarrow, into which flew a lighted firework, igniting the whole collection with an instantaneous, spectacular, unchoreographed display.

Those within the safety of the building came closer to the display than they anticipated as at least one rocket flew into a dormitory. Thankfully, neither human nor building was damaged.

Schools of that size, 150–200, have always needed careful management, especially in the last thirty years with inflationary pressures, staff salaries, pension contributions, facility development and so on. The loss or gain of a few pupils has significant financial implications. Richard Jennings, the new Head, had warmth, charisma and passion for his school, where pastoral care had equal value to academic, musical, artistic, sporting and co-curricular achievement. The community grew in size and strength, including boarding numbers, the school being relatively close to the naval base at Portsmouth and not so far from army bases.

Military families benefited from what is now called the Continuity of Education Allowance. If posted from station to station, their children could attend a boarding school with the fees heavily subsidised. Such allowances have since been substantially curtailed over the years and very much to the detriment of smaller boarding schools. For Great Ballard at that time, however, it was a huge boon. This was a happy community and parents within the army or navy shared their positive experiences with colleagues, who then sent their own children.

When all seemed to be going so well, the school's owners fell upon hard times and a new proprietor was desperately sought. For me personally, it felt like history repeating, somewhat groundhog, but for the Head it must have been devastating and deeply concerning, having invested his family, young children and future in the school.

Around that time a family had approached the school as prospective parents regarding their son, who was disabled. They had been turned away from a number of other independent schools and were desperate for a caring environment for their young child. A measure of the character, Richard wanted to see if he could make it work. The parents offered to pay for any measures needed to enable access and the son joined the school – a kind and fortuitous decision as the grandfather bought the school. It remains under family ownership today with continuing, considerable investment.

Having done some acting at school, I added drama to my teaching portfolio, directing plays annually. Again, possibly naïve, my ambitions and expectations may have exceeded the norm for the 13+ age group, which became a deliberate choice later in my career; I adopted the mantra, 'expect little of children, they will disappoint – expect much and they will surprise.' As a theatre-goer I enjoyed Oscar Wilde, Bernard Shaw, Molière and Goldoni. Whether just fortunate in the talents of the pupils at the time – Honeysuckle Weeks being one – or through considered casting, a series of successful plays followed. Honeysuckle went on to later fame on stage and screen, perhaps best known for her part in *Foyle's War* with Michael Kitchen. The most memorable production was *The Importance of Being Earnest*, where the cast came to understand the language and wit while enjoying the farce, their timing of lines far exceeding their years.

Miles Malleson's translations of Moliere's plays and Goldoni's *Servant of Two Masters* came in future years. The hall and stage were small, the lighting and staging unsophisticated, but the intensity and intimacy of the performances provided an experience for some that was formative in their development: learning lines, following direction, working as a team, reacting and responding when things went wrong – which of course they did and with some style.

By this time I was Head of English, boarding house tutor, sports coach and drama teacher; variety being the spice of Prep School life. The school was busy, thriving and happy. As I write I am looking at a brass plaque mounted on a wooden base, engraved 'Mr. Piercy from the 1st XI 1991'. That season the football team had beaten the formidable Westbourne House. I would take the U11 cricketers to St. Aubyn's, Rottingdean, high on the cliffs above the English Channel, playing through horizontal rain urged by chilling gusts, returning to boarding duties in the evening. Saturday mornings saw academic lessons with sports fixtures in the afternoon and Sundays, trips to the coast or up onto the South Downs. The children would enjoy the space, the grounds and the woods, with tree climbing permitted in those days. The Head even created a formidable par-three golf course on The Mound, pupils, parents and colleagues digging, levelling and sowing. One Sunday the fire alarm sounded and there was indeed a fire in the cellar – thankfully, quickly extinguished. Never again was I comfortable or even complacent at the sounding of an alarm.

Having turned thirty and beginning to feel a bit like an adult, the time was approaching when some more serious career thinking had to be done. For reasons no longer known, I saw an advertisement in *The Sunday Times* for a recruitment consultant and applied. To my astonishment I was invited for interview in London, which must have gone well as I was called back. The partner said the skills they required were comparable with those of a teacher. Perhaps fortuitously the process went no further, fate drawing me in, but it did have the effect of reinforcing my career choice to date and affirming some ambition to progress.

In a further spur to professional ambition, I was now married with a delightful baby daughter. We lived in a lovely but rather cramped apartment on the second floor of the Lutyens house. Those who are parents will understand the paraphernalia that accompanies parenthood, from big bags of nappies to car seats, prams and strollers. It was time to try and career further up that ladder.

SENIOR MANAGEMENT

School inspections assess on two counts: achievement and personal development. The two undeniably go hand in hand and every teacher must be equally conscious of both. When moving from middle to senior management a choice often has to be made: curriculum leadership or pastoral care. An advert in the *Times Educational Supplement* caught my eye: Director of Studies at Forres Sandle Manor – now known as 'FSM'. This was a traditional, boarding, rural Prep School on the edge of Fordingbridge near the New Forest in Hampshire. I wasn't conscious at the time of the relevance of this position, which became apparent later in my career. Forres in Swanage, Dorset and Sandle Manor, Fordingbridge, had recently merged. The Head was young, dynamic, characterful and employed me.

One of the youngest ever to take up Headship in a Prep School, his energy and enthusiasm were infectious – as was his delightfully politically incorrect sense of humour. A piece of his advice for leading a school stayed with me, with much greater understanding when a Head:

'the first half of term is for doing; the second half for surviving'. Fellow Heads will recognise the way a term hurtles towards the end, colleagues tiring, increasingly brittle, stamina beginning to dwindle. One thinks of those partitions in the hull of the *Titanic* that, when breached, allowed water to cascade through the ship, tipping and sinking. In a similar vein, I would later refer to 'start-of-term conversations' – some things best delayed until such times when bodies and minds are fresher.

I was the first senior appointment independent of both schools and therein lay the challenge – for the Head and thus for me, too: knitting together two common rooms and blending both into one, homogenous ethos. The location was again beneficial for pupil recruitment, with the naval base and the military establishments of Salisbury and Andover close by, both of which sustained boarding numbers. With more recent headwinds, socio-political and economic turbulence, mergers, takeovers and independent school consortia are increasingly common – and common sense. This merge, however, was prescient and considerably ahead of its time.

My first academic initiative was to look at the handwriting policy. Why this I cannot specifically recall, though it did happen to be an area of personal interest. The primary school days when a misguided teacher had tried to make me write right-handed had long-lasting consequences. I had tried to learn golf as a left-hander – subsequently, less miserably, moving to right-handed clubs. On the cricket field I would bowl left-handed and bat right-handed and there is a school of thought which reinforces the logic of this, with the left shoulder leading.

As a dedicated cack-hander, many a pupil has asked why I write upside down or sideways. The reason lies in the angle of the page. The right-hander should angle the page some forty-five degrees anti-clockwise, the left-hander forty-five degrees clockwise. This important factor had somehow escaped me and, learning to write with a fountain pen, I effectively smudged or wiped out everything I had written; hence I angled the wrist and wrote from above. The answer quite probably lies in the teaching at St. Saviour's School, Lagos. It is reassuring and affirming when I see others writing in a similar manner and has often been an amusing conversation with pupils: 'Sir, why do you write upside down?' My writing on a whiteboard has been another source of entertainment for children, as has their interpretation of my indecipherable scrawl.

I had little idea what I was letting myself in for, what I was unleashing, by questioning a handwriting policy, something I thought would be easily achieved through discussion and consultation. How wrong I was. The statement, 'But we've always done it this way,' begs the response, 'Why? Have you never questioned whether there might be an alternative – possibly better – way?' The sort of critical thinking we encourage in our pupils.

Teachers at the lower end of the school were wedded (welded) to what they had been doing, seemingly forever, since the days of the quill. The Learning Support department was keen to adopt a cursive scheme, which those who wished to adhere to their original semi-cursive programme considered loopy – literally and metaphorically. To my surprise there was considerable heat in the debate – an early lesson in broaching change, questioning, challenging long-standing practice. There's a lovely, apocryphal story of a new Head who on his first day, having delivered the first assembly, wanders the school, has various meetings, then disappears to the safety and seclusion of his study. Feeling a little hungry, he emerges and asks the secretary the time of lunch to the response, 'Lunch is at 1pm, Headmaster. It has always been at 1 o'clock; we like it at 1 o'clock.'

Those central to teaching handwriting would meet and we considered a variety of schemes. Gradually there was an acceptance of change but what eventually emerged was an exciting hybrid of styles – our own FSM Handwriting Scheme. Colin Powell, soldier, statesman and diplomat, oft quoted on leadership, puts it well: '…never lose sight of the need to reach out and talk to other people who don't share your view. Listen to them and see if you can find a way to compromise.' This does not mean having to sacrifice fundamental principles and, in this instance, all parties were eventually satisfied with the outcome (at least that's what they said to my face). Some months after the new scheme had been introduced, the Head of Junior School came to find me, showing a child's work: beautiful, cursive handwriting of which she was clearly proud.

We can all recall certain teachers who had more powerful influences on us as pupils, my A Level Maths teacher being a prime example. Another, a young master at Prep School, took us all outside to learn *La Marseillaise* – French teaching had never been so stimulating. The same applies to teachers with their memories of individual pupils – for better or for worse, in both cases. I recall three delightful rogues: A, B and C. A was, by any Year 8 standards, a BFG of prop-forward proportions. He had character to match – larger than life. He found academic work something of a burden – not quite the Spadge Hopkins of Laurie's Lee's *Cider with Rosie*, grunting, groaning and squirming at his desk but not a million miles removed. It was humour, a big, easy smile, a natural affability and resilience which got him through.

B was dyslexic and had ADHD, and bore the family tragedy of a father who had taken his own life – bigger burdens than we can truly understand. B was often in trouble and generally (but delightfully) chaotic: work not done, late, answering back and arguing with teachers. A misguided teacher put a 'D' on the cover of the exercise books of those who were dyslexic to remind him of their dyslexia when marking their work. One is reminded of the dunce cap which, although not his intention, was to those affected a stigmatising label. C was also dyslexic – seriously so. It was my privilege to teach him English. C was bright, perceptive, shrewd and, orally at least, highly articulate with a lovely turn of phrase. Today he would have a reader and extra time; then he was fortunate to have a brilliant learning support teacher but not always great understanding or empathy from all.

These three good friends operated as something of a pack though absolutely not in a predatory way.

Reminiscent of the musketeers, they leant on the boundaries of convention with a certain charm. They also grew into greater self-awareness in Year 8, as do many 13+ pupils at Prep School. The emotional and conceptual differences between an eleven- and thirteen-year-old are immense. The Prep School 13+ model, like the state Middle School, which is still applicable in a few counties, works – especially for boys. When the trio left at the end of Year 8 I was given a small framed photo of them all, shoulder to shoulder, arms around each other, with the (handwritten, just legible) inscription, 'When you think you've had a bad day…'

Our daughter was two when our second child, a son, was born. We had started at FSM in a flat in the main building but with two children, more space was needed. We moved to a house in the grounds – a mere hundred metres from the main building but graced with space and a small garden. Around that time, we bought our own home in the delightful market town of Hatherleigh in North Devon (soon after of Mad Cow Disease fame) finding a life away from work and school in a happy, diverse community. The Old Church House, although a little run down, was a delightful, quirky refuge overlooking the graveyard and reputedly formerly The Priest's House, with stories of a tunnel connecting with the church – never discovered or excavated.

Three enjoyable years were spent at FSM. It was a happy, productive place with a warming sense of community, in part due to the strength of boarding. Schools with a boarding element – no matter in what proportion to day pupils – have a different feel. Good boarding schools should feel like a home from home, especially in the Prep sector. Summer weekends saw barbecues, swimming (in the outdoor pool), walks in the New Forest, trips to the coast and soapy, slippery water slides down the bank at the back of the school.

There I would have remained but for the tug of two temptations. I realised at this stage I did indeed wish to make that final step upwards to Headship and was duly enrolled on the IAPS (Independent Association of Prep Schools) 'Aspiring Heads' Course' held at Jesus College, Oxford, Easter 1998. This was the closest I would ever get to an Oxbridge college and it felt something of a privilege. Run by the Chair and Director of Education at IAPS, my memory is of a course designed to test the will and stamina of candidates while raising awareness of the complexities that come with running a school. Bursars blinded us with budgets and accounting; serving heads told horror stories setting situational scenarios; lawyers just terrified us all. One scenario asked how a Head would manage the community perception of a family with same-sex parents joining the school. Society's acceptance of diversity in whatever form has thankfully come a long way in the last twenty-five years.

Temptation one was a return to Africa. Having been born in Tanzania, but with only vague, limited memories as we moved to Nigeria when I was four, we had been on holiday to Kenya before the children were born. We started in Nairobi and then made that legendary overnight rail journey – which is no more – taking us to Mombasa.

The railway has since been modernised but in the mid-1990s it remained as it may well have done since colonial days. The rolling stock was tired, as were the waiters' uniforms, though still retaining their full, immaculate, gleaming white livery and frayed gloves. The train moved ponderously and noisily from temperate Nairobi, gathering mosquitoes as it descended its rattling way to tropical Mombasa, the train tracks and sleepers clearly visible when looking down the loo. Waking as dawn broke and the train rolled through Tsavo, children ran alongside cheering and calling to the passengers, with Kilimanjaro visible, its head shrouded in cloud.

When in Nairobi we visited a number of Prep Schools as one career ambition was to live and work in East Africa. The 'big one' is The Banda but for some reason a tour of the school wasn't achievable in such a short visit. An appointment was successfully made to see Kenton College Prep School. Our arrival felt somewhat inauspicious, seeing queues of staff who seemed a little disgruntled. We learned later they had been disputing their pay. It was a distinctive tour: a Kenyan Prep School which seemed to have been magically transplanted from the UK home counties – even the dining-room felt and smelt familiar. Although we visited in the school holidays, the impression was still of a slice of traditional Britain.

The second visit was to Peponi House in a suburb of Nairobi. Unlike Kenton College this was – is – a day school, and it caught the eye with its aura of energy and some impressive facilities. As it happened this was to be the first foray into Headship applications when, in my third year at

FSM, the position was advertised. The temptation was not to be resisted and I applied. First-round interviews were to be held at Cumberland Lodge in Windsor Great Park – grand surroundings indeed – just after the end of the summer term. Whether due to the fact it took place the night after the end-of-year staff party played a part, or I was the wrong character, or just underprepared for such a crucial interview, my application was taken no further.

It seems the majority of Headship appointments are now conducted by recruitment specialists, 'headhunters', which is wise for such a key role. The Peponi experience, however, was extraordinary and a lesson not just for this candidate but also in how to conduct an interview process – or not. It took place in a large reception room at a table that must have been more than six metres long. The panel (of five?) was spread across the length of the table with someone at each end, the candidate immediately at a disadvantage in trying to capture the interest of all panellists – not least a member of the prestigious Kenyatta family. Whether deliberate or careless, such a scenario is unlikely to bring out the best for anyone involved, above all a nervous candidate. An interview should provide the best, safest opportunity for a candidate to demonstrate his/her capabilities and suitability for the position advertised.

The second temptation was Dunhurst, Bedales' Prep School in Hampshire. The Headship had been advertised a year earlier – too early for me, thus I was pleased to see it appear again in my third year at FSM.

John Badley, the founder of Bedales, was a pioneer, a visionary, a man ahead of his time. He sought to break away from the traditions, the shackles of the British Public School system, with an ethos which was progressive and, in my view, enlightened. Initially boys only, there had been less emphasis on the classics and what he saw as the constraints or limitations of a British academic education. Rugby was eschewed (Badley had attended Rugby School from age fifteen) and 'outdoor work' was part of the curriculum, something that continues today with farming and smallholding. In a further progression at the turn of the nineteenth and twentieth centuries, Badley had broken the public school mould by making Bedales the first co-educational boarding school, which was by then settled in Steep, Petersfield, where it thrives today, a stunning arts and crafts building at its centre. If you drive along a particular road near Hayward's Heath you will see a house sign 'Bedales', which is where the school was originally founded.

While Badley himself had been quite authoritarian, he created an ethos which at the time – and even now – is quite different. Read many a school motto or mission statement and try to discern difference: most schools profess to do the same things. His mantra of 'head, hand, heart', where there was a spiritual but non-denominational education, was ground-breaking – and has since been 'borrowed' by other schools. I was attracted to a school which was liberal and progressive; where there was no uniform; where pupils called teachers by their first names. With hindsight (being quite a traditionalist at heart) this seems curious. Emerging was a philosophy that bespoke, individual pastoral care, kindness and mutual respect were central to a child's happiness and development, and therefore effective, holistic education.

Alison Willcocks was Head of the Senior School at the time and it was she, with a governor selection panel, who managed the interview process. A central element when appointing staff, no matter their role, is about a meeting of minds, a human connection – psychometric testing can expose only so much. I recall little of the interview process, which probably reveals a great deal, a genuine coalescing of characters and educational philosophy. At the age of thirty-five I was thrilled and excited to be offered the job.

HEADSHIP

No matter how comprehensive the preparation, training, MEd, NPQH or experience, the step up from Senior Team to Headship is immeasurable. As a senior member of staff or Deputy there is always a backstop, someone to whom you can pass the question, problem or buck. As Head – and especially of a Prep School as opposed to a Senior School – every decision is yours: from the blocked toilet to staff discipline. A Prep School Head must expect to get dirty hands and be seen to do so. A good, supportive Chair of Governors and board is essential and they are there to listen, counsel, mentor and possibly coach, but they are not operational. Decisions remain with you. A first Headship in a Prep attached to a Senior School provides security and support – though the lure of applying for something freestanding, 'running your own show', is very tempting.

To follow the Aspiring Heads' course, IAPS stipulated attendance of the Heads' Induction Course, this time held at beautiful Canford School in Dorset. The Head of FSM had led this course in previous years and perhaps it was a good thing he was not in charge on this occasion – entertaining though it would have been. Based on his own experience of a particular incident, I remember him telling me to try and always have two exits from the Head's study. He was once caught climbing out of his office window into a flowerbed to avoid an encounter with a difficult parent approaching with menace down the narrow corridor. As with the preliminary course, which had tested our collective resolve, the imminent, impending Heads were all once again in awe of what we had let ourselves in for by taking up Headship.

I recall questioning one piece of advice in particular. It was suggested incoming Heads should ask for pictures of all pupils so they could learn everyone's name before starting. I baulked at this for two reasons. Firstly, it is not how my brain works; I would simply not retain the information. The second is more profound as, to my mind, it seems a little contrived, artificial and mechanical. Knowing the face and name does not mean knowing the person behind the face; the character, strength, frailty, foible. If you know them you can read them – their expression and body language.

Is everyone a 'people watcher'? Much of this writing is done while in the bizarre and beautiful city of Venice – 'La Serenissima' – having stood down from Headship after serving a total of twenty-five years across three very different schools. A time to reflect. Wandering the *calli* and *fondamenti* of Venice I pass by people of all nations, shapes and sizes. A face that may appear grumpy or cheery does not necessarily indicate character or state of mind;

the face may just be built that way. That said, a warm smile with both mouth and eyes lights up the face.

Education is a human business where relationships underpin everything from achievement and success to happiness. In 2020, at the outset of the Covid pandemic – much more of which later – we abruptly lost the familiarity, the taken-for-granted human contact. At the time I was Head of The New Beacon, a boys' Prep School in Sevenoaks. I began writing a weekly 'blog' (for want of a better word) entitled 'Reflections', a view on matters in school, education or the wider world.

Reflections: an extract from 22.5.20

We talk of the positive things which can emerge from our current challenges, one of which is developing the ability to adapt. The workplace has become increasingly complex and fluid in recent years and Covid-19 will add to that sense of churn: remote working, the use of technology, economic uncertainty. The notion of a remote school was unthinkable just a few short months ago yet we have learnt to adapt with considerable agility.

Our remoteness has brought into sharp focus the importance of humanity in a school – relationships: between boys and boys, between boys and teachers; the power of a community, the whole being greater than the sum of parts. I have seen nearly all the boys in various assemblies today and also my colleagues. The sense of community has been palpable. Therein lies my pride: congratulations to all and have a restful half term – well deserved!

Reflections 20.11.21

The theme in assembly yesterday was bullying, as one might expect in anti-bullying week. Bullying is a word bandied around in schools all the time (quite rightly) from the earliest of ages. I asked the boys for their understanding of the word. Many hands shot up with the immediate response of 'repeated' and 'deliberate' unkindness. They know. We then talked about 'banter' – slightly more fragile territory.

Here I must make a confession. I engage in banter with the older boys. Not persistently, not regularly and certainly not unkindly but I do sometimes tease them. I can do so because I know them; their foibles and frailties. And they know I am joking. The same understanding cannot always be said of children themselves who have not yet developed the emotional maturity and awareness of others' sensitivities.

I talk to the boys about 'reading the signals' – the body language, the facial expressions of others. A 'banterish' word on one day may be taken as an unkind word on another and our job as adults is to engender that empathic skill of sensing others' feelings; their frame of mind. Banter is not necessarily bullying – neither persistent nor deliberately unkind – but can cause hurt. For the children the lesson in life is to notice and be sensitive to their peers' emotional equilibrium.

The Heads' Induction Course was productive and informative. Thereafter, I think we all tracked each others' progress over the years as we careered through one or more schools. A few of us sustained very close friendships – the Class of '98 – which remains strong today. The sharing of successes, experiences, trials and tribulations softens the sometimes isolation of Headship. While there is much camaraderie amongst Heads within the various IAPS districts, these colleagues are also competitors – it is easier to share challenges and anecdotes with friends out of the district.

As we move further into the twenty-first century, it is clear the pressures the independent sector has increasingly faced in recent years are likely to intensify. I avoid the word 'exponentially' when mentioning Covid, the economy and socio-political antipathy all conspiring against us. I was struck by a comment piece from Laura Thompson in *The Telegraph*: 'Posh people or people with immaculate accents or people who own Labradors are about the only 'minority' that can be attacked with impunity.' The extraordinary thing is the prescience of this comment written so long ago in September 2014.

Alison Willcocks provided a listening, critical ear through, as a minimum, weekly meetings. She was measured, calm and experienced. Dunhurst had been under consistent leadership, a steady hand, for many years. Alison had been Deputy at Bedales, internally promoted to Headship. She recognised the need for change – evolution, not revolution. This, she felt, also applied to Dunhurst. I was given the freedom to consider the strengths, weaknesses, opportunities and threats, which I later had to present to the governing board with Alison's full support. At the same time I recalled the wise words of a parent at FSM, a senior military officer, who advised, 'The only thing you should change in your first year is the angle of your desk.' When succeeding a long-standing, well-regarded Head, this is good advice indeed. Ideally, a full academic year needs to be under the belt to get a deeper understanding of the subtleties and nuances of how a school works.

Bedales – and thus Dunhurst – attracted something of a celebrity clientele. Many were from the world of the arts and based in London. Petersfield has increasingly become a commuter town, just an hour or so from London Waterloo, providing a strong market for day places. In the mid-nineties, and even more so today, Prep School boarding was a fiercely competitive and diminishing market. It struck me that more work could be done to attract boys and girls from London day schools. A strategic goal was to produce a marketing campaign to meet this aim, followed by visits to targeted London Preps. There followed visits of some of those Heads to Dunhurst.

Bedales has a certain reputational mythology. Prospective parents, shown round by Dunhurst's Year 8 boys and girls, were known to ask, seriously but with incredulity, if pupils were allowed to drink, smoke and even take drugs: a clear misunderstanding of that liberal, progressive ethos. This was only the late 1990s.

To those who had not done their due diligence, and even to the initiated, the school certainly seemed very different with no uniform and the informal (yet clearly respectful) relations between pupils and staff. While one might think the lack of uniform would inexorably lead to something of a cheque book-labelled fashion show, this was not the case. The theme at the time was very much denim, dungarees and 'grunge'. One Head of a particularly smart London Prep, surprised on arrival at the lack of uniform, commented after his tour that Dunhurst was in fact more structured than his own school. The informality was a sleight of hand since, as with any school, the atmosphere must be dependent on a culture of respect – pupil for teacher and teacher for pupil.

A fine tradition of Dunhurst was 'Jaw', which took place on a Friday evening in a central space called 'The Well', a hub around which were classrooms. It had a series of steps across its breadth where pupils sat for the formal end of the week. 'Jaw' was a talk, most often by a visiting speaker. The theme could be anything from factual, educational and experiential to moral or spiritual. Jaw finished with all the teachers lining up at the bottom of The Well; each child would walk the line, shaking everyone's hand. Whatever had passed during the busy week, this was a moment of mutual respect and, sometimes, reconciliation.

Reflections 5.11.21

We're not sure what to do any more. An article in The Sunday Times *last week struck a chord reflecting on the tradition of the handshake – we all recognise the uncertainty of a greeting in 2021.*

Pre-Prep and Junior School Celebration Assembly is a highlight of the week – always so much to recognise and applaud. I never fail to be impressed by our boys who respond so well to direction and training: on receipt of an award, eye contact, perhaps a smile, thank you and a handshake. For a brief time we resorted to the elbow bump. One boy who was so thrilled to have won the Courtesy Cup looked me in the eye, said thank you, and was so enthusiastic in his elbow bump that pain went shooting up my arm and lingered for hours.

This morning, as usual, the Courtesy Cup and Shield were presented. The tradition is for the award and certificate to be raised on high, akin to the FA Cup. This morning the joy of the winners was palpable – as was the enthusiastic applause from everyone else. The Golden Book recognises a range of achievement; names are read out along with the achievement. Today we had persistence, handwriting (pen licence awarded!), efficiency, 100% effort all the time, reading and maths, resilience and progress. One of my favourites – a key skill to develop in boys: completing work quickly AND accurately; two aspects which don't always go hand-in-hand.

My favourite, however, is kindness and care for others, which brings us back to the handshake and courtesy. The handshake is making an uncertain return but the sentiments which lie behind remain constant: the warmth of greeting and friendship.

One of the most memorable talks was given by Mo Mowlam, on occasion a controversial politician, who can be credited with successfully helping to reach the Good Friday Agreement in Northern Ireland. She 'cut through conventions and made difficult decisions that gave momentum to political progress' (Peter Hain, 2005, Wikipedia). Already suffering from a brain tumour and hair loss, there was no diminution of eloquence or intelligence and, as one might hope, there were many questions from the pupils. Neither Bedales nor Dunhurst had any religious practice but Jaw provided a plethora of views and perspectives, giving a strong spiritual education and awareness of the wider world.

Another celebrity parent was Pete Townshend – of The Who fame. He was in my experience a very decent man of considerable, admirable humility. The school was having its biennial parents' ball and seeking donations to auction for charity. The Who had a reunion tour in the late nineties. Relatively unsolicited and with great generosity, Pete donated return flights to New York on Concorde, backstage passes and five-star hotel accommodation. Somewhere around that time I was in a supermarket in Petersfield when a gentleman approached as I stood in front of the salad counter. 'Hello, Mike.' Looking up, I thought I saw the Head of Design Technology from the Senior School, smiled and replied, 'Hello Martin.' The gentleman looked a little confused. It quickly dawned on me I was talking to none other than Pete Townshend. 'Gosh, I'm so sorry, Pete.' I explained and apologised for the mistaken identity. 'Not at all; perfectly understandable out of context.' There followed a brief, pleasant chat about his son.

There were many children in Dunhurst who were brimming with confidence, which, it has to be said, occasionally bubbled over the brim of acceptability.

As with a proportion of children privileged to attend independent schools, there was an aura around some individuals that life came waiter-served on a bone china plate with finest silver cutlery – a sense of entitlement. There were of course those whose parents were making enormous sacrifices to pay school fees, as there are in all schools. There were also many children who lacked confidence, who were unassuming and far removed from that sense of entitlement.

One girl springs to mind. In stature she was small for her age, bespectacled, and would generally only speak to adults when encouraged or asked a direct question. For a teacher there is a risk that such children can be missed, flying below the radar. One day her teacher asked her to play in assembly – the oboe, a phenomenally difficult instrument from which to elicit a good, clear, stable sound. It was a stunning performance, beautifully controlled with dynamics that belied her age. Deservedly, it met with rapturous applause – she seemed to grow, visibly, before us. It was no surprise when I heard she had proceeded to a conservatoire.

In my second year at Dunhurst the building works began, having already presented to Alison Willcocks and the governors what I felt to be the strategic aims of the school. The investment of large sums of money into what I felt to be the future of the school was a heavy responsibility. There were two elements: classrooms and a junior boarding wing. Neither project was simple as the main school building was on sloping ground and to the rear there was a steep bank where the new boarding wing would be. The school was growing, hence more classrooms were needed – and also to reinforce subject-specific areas in Years 7 and 8. The junior boarding wing for eight- to eleven-year-olds was built in anticipation of the hopefully growing numbers of parents sending their children to weekly board at a younger age, while also giving the older boarders a sense of independence, seniority and privilege.

Effective running of meetings – allowing debate and dissent then bringing matters to a conclusion – is a skill learnt only through practice, trial and error. There was a weekly staff meeting with an open agenda. I recall one occasion when I think I was being put to the test – as will often be the case for a new Head. In the early days of Headship, one wants to be seen to be clear-thinking and decisive. The question raised was one about the girls' attire. With no rules about clothing and uniform, it wasn't unusual for the older girls to tend to the minimalist in their wardrobe choice, causing discomfort for some staff, male and female. There was a fundamental Badleyan principle which dictated the freedom for the pupils to choose their own clothing, to express their individuality, yet there was also the matter of staff levels of comfort.

The debate bounced backwards and forwards from the defenders of the faith to the more conservative. Time was running out, break nearly over, with lessons to attend and children in classrooms, and a decision had to be reached. Upholding the principle of freedom of choice, two provisos were decided upon: girls' clothing should neither offend decency nor compromise safety. The safety element is easy to justify; the decency subjective, thus less so. One person's definition of 'decency' is different to another's. The responsibility was placed with the staff: if they felt uncomfortable with a girl's clothing, if it offended the individual, they should tell the child. This was put to the school at the next gathering with a full explanation of the rationale. While there may well have been some adolescent mutterings, it was accepted that staff had the right to respect just as much as the pupils.

My first child had been born when we lived in a top-floor flat at Great Ballard; the second when at FSM, where I had been promoted to Deputy Head while running the boarding house – albeit with a very good resident tutor and team of staff. Marriages fail for many reasons but one, I am sure in my case, is taking on such burdensome responsibilities at a relatively young age and with very young children.

Boarding schools are all-consuming with long days, nights and weekends. React strongly if someone suggests teachers have an easy life. Yes, there are the holidays, but that does not compensate for lost time with family, young children, bath, bed and story times. With a failed marriage, separation and divorce in process, some time was needed to reflect and recalibrate. With great sadness, I stood down from leading Dunhurst after three productive, generally happy and probably formative years, retreating to our house in Devon.

On leaving Dunhurst, a profoundly emotional departure, I was given the clear impression by the then-Bedales Head that a Prep Head needs to be married. Such a suggestion was certainly inappropriate and deeply disheartening at the time. It is quite shocking today. With a background and experience in boarding education, his premise was, however, something which had to be borne in mind (though perhaps best not articulated). Which jobs might I seek and what might the future hold? My ideal was a country, freestanding Prep and while I was offended by the suggestion of the Bedales Head, I knew there was substance to what he had implied. The traditional model is of a Prep School website front page image of a young, smiley couple, at least a brace of children and, ideally, a Labrador or similar. My children were living with their mother, I was single and I had no dog.

Meanwhile, the house in Hatherleigh, Devon, was something of a refuge. I needed time to ponder and reposition; to try and reassemble what felt like the fragments of my life and career. Those who have experienced divorce will empathise with the pain and trauma, especially where children are involved. Once again it was a parent who gave words of wisdom: when your personal life is in turmoil, focus on the professional – and vice versa.

The sixteenth-century, delightfully dilapidated, house would need to be sold as part of the divorce settlement. Some DIY work had to be done, which I enjoyed and was somehow therapeutic. Just off the sitting room, up a couple of steps, was an under-used, quite sizeable room in which there was a curiously, somewhat eccentrically, located loo with a view over the beautiful churchyard; the space having little purpose otherwise. I decided to put up a partition and create a shower room, working only from the tome of a DIY manual.

I was pleased with progress: 'four by two' timber framework, plasterboard panelling and then the challenge of plastering. I expect we have all seen newly plastered rooms at some point – it is an underrated art, leaving walls clean and smooth: perfectionism, patience, attention to detail. In a sixteenth-century house where nothing was true or even, 'one-coat' plaster was the answer, leaving a rustic finish and potentially manageable for a true amateur. All was going well until, having foolishly left the bucket of plaster at the bottom of the ladder, I descended, placing my boot firmly in the bucket – prolonged, solitary laughter at the comic book scene.

FAITH

As the French would say, '*Bon courage!*' We talk to children about managing failure or disappointment: falling off the bicycle, getting up, dusting off, climbing back on and pedalling away. Over the years it has been a worry to see a growing culture of error avoidance, risk-averse education; 'everyone's a winner'. 'One who makes no mistakes makes nothing.' Most, if not all, of us face crises in our lives, turning points, crossroads. If we do not learn to acknowledge these, then how do we learn to rebuild?

Reflections 2.10.20

There is much chat amongst the boys (and staff) about the new football season – playing to desolate stadia yet still plenty of excitement.

Who would have thought it – Everton at the top of the Premiership (if only just for a few hours); Leicester now top and Man Utd 14th? Early days, I know, but as an Evertonian, it's a great start to the season. I talk to the boys about 'disappointment' rather than 'failure'. The *former allows reflection on what led to disappointment, whether it be unrealistic expectation, the competition too great, or inadequate preparation. The latter, failure, is rather more damning. I use my support for Everton as a positive illustration of disappointment: it can make us more resilient with a growth mindset.*

Reflections 3.2.23

Although we may not yet be out of the woods, the mornings and evenings are discernibly lighter – the boys will soon be able to unpin those armbands! There has been a whiff of spring this week: the birdsong in the mornings is joyous and uplifting.

January can be a bit of a flat month. Christmas, Chinese New Year and festivity are seemingly behind us and hibernation is perhaps what we are meant to be doing. It is all the more impressive therefore to see boys clambering out of cars every morning, happy to be in school – witnessing one Y1 boy running across the Garden Pitch to get to his classroom this week.

The theme in chapel this evening for Y7/8 was around the subject of 'perspective'. On occasion in this piece I will refer to the fact that we talk more about disappointment in school rather than failure. We can rationalise disappointment. Such an approach is not ill-concealed political correctness; it is about developing a growth mindset, seeking and finding the positives.

The first step back onto the career ladder was the *Times Educational Supplement*. What was currently being advertised? I also renewed contact with the recruitment agencies where our paths had crossed in the past. While there may have been others, the one that caught my eye was Moor Park, Ludlow, a Catholic Prep School just outside Ludlow. The website showed a magnificent Queen Anne country house set in acres of parkland in stunning South Shropshire. This was a region unknown to me and would present challenges, with my children based in Sussex, but it was worth a go. I clambered back onto my bike and set the application wheels in motion.

The Catholicity was an interesting and appealing aspect of Moor Park. My mother had been a devout Catholic. While my father was probably agnostic, taking no part in religious practice, as children we attended Mass regularly in Falomo, Lagos, with our mother. I recall a barn of a building that was always full, hot, airless and humid. My brother and I were both christened into the Catholic church, had our first Holy Communion at Falomo, and were confirmed in a half-built cathedral in Apapa by, I believe, the Archbishop of Lagos.

My mother was an extraordinary woman. Born in 1920 in County Sligo, she left Ireland to join her step-sister in London, training as a nurse and serving in the Blitz. That one, simple sentence conceals much to surprise for the first half of the twentieth century and possibly even today. Firstly, a step-sister. My mother's father – who I never met – was legendary in their small town. Even today he is remembered for various reasons, most of which being dubious. He was a sometime mayor, publican and 'enforcer' (possibly debt or rent collecting) known to arrive and knock on someone's door carrying what might have been a knobkerrie or shillelagh. He had a daughter by his first marriage and when his wife died he remarried, producing two further daughters and a son. It is the son who is remembered in particular for being bullied by his father. Someone recalled him cutting grass with a pair of scissors. He left Ireland for Merseyside to escape his father, sadly dying far too young.

My mother never forgave her father for this, returning to Ireland only rarely to see her sister and step-sister. She believed her father with his bullying ways had been responsible for her brother's early death, something she only told me in her seventies, tongue-loosened and fortified by white wine.

In London she lived and worked through the Blitz. Though she rarely spoke of that time, she did talk about evacuating the ward and moving patients into the nearby underground station. From London as a military nurse – and then Ward Sister – my mother travelled post-war Europe, and through North Africa to Tanzania. The army must have provided security but the independence and spirit she showed were remarkable for the time. She always said she never intended to marry; a plan that changed when she met my father in Dar es Salaam, Tanzania.

In spite of what must have been a traumatic childhood and youth, she never lost or questioned her faith; indeed, it strengthened in later life. After my father died the church was central to her very being. As I watched the priest administering to her the last rites at ninety-seven years of age, dementia having taken its toll, the sincerity, the power of her lucid gaze, locking into my tearful eyes, revealed clarity, understanding and peace. As for me, though I wished I had that depth of faith, I was not constant in my Catholic practice – which is not to say I rejected it. Being Catholic, as declared on the application form for Moor Park, was clearly a plus. Being single and divorced was, I feared, a potential minus. I proceeded with the application nonetheless.

Most job applications today are done online, which was not generally the case at the end of the twentieth century – just as well, since I had no technology in the house. In those early days of Headship, when advertising a teaching position I used to ask for a handwritten letter to accompany the application, until someone asked if I used the handwriting for some form of psychological analysis. The application form and related paperwork, job, school description and person specification duly arrived by post. It also included a psychometric test, which I completed with some anxiety and haste in my car outside the Hatherleigh Post Office. Am I the only one when completing such tasks who tries to second guess which might be the right answers without necessarily doing some deep, personal navel gazing?

The psychometric test and application form completed, the papers went into the post and I waited, delighted some days later to get a phone call inviting me for interview. The drive up the M5 was smooth and, arriving early, I dropped into Ludlow, just a few miles from the school. Ludlow is utterly enchanting and, at the time, was the gastro capital of the UK. An emphasis on home-grown and home-produced had attracted a series of chefs and gastronomers to follow. The town teemed with independent boutique shops, artisan bakers, butchers and delicatessens. I had forgotten my cufflinks and bought some in a smart gift shop, which I later discovered belonged to a future Chair of Governors. Suitably equipped, crossing the River Teme and climbing towards the Mortimer Forest, I drove to the school in nearby Richard's Castle.

The entrance from the Leominster Road is imposing in itself, as was fitting for a fine country house. It was built in mid-seventeenth century by the Salwey family and held by them until the late nineteenth century. It is a stately building, arguably best viewed from the road above, giving a panorama of the red-brick structure within parkland and, today, expansive sports fields laid out in front. The cricket square must have one of the most beautiful settings in the country. The estate has a rich history, including being the home for evacuated Lancing College, Sussex, in the Second World War. Tom Sharpe was a boarder at the time, using the building and some of the owning family for the inspiration and setting of *Blott on the Landscape*.

The school as it is today was founded by Messrs Hugh Watts and Derek Henderson in 1964. Both had been first-class cricketers and taught at Downside School. They wished to model their school on the best examples of traditional Prep Schools such as Ludgrove, bringing with them the Catholicity and Benedictine principles of Downside. It rapidly gained momentum and reputation as a top-performing Prep School, attracting families from

London and across the country, competing with other, longer-standing, prestigious establishments.

By the time I came on the scene, Hugh Watts had passed away. I did at various stages meet Ursula Watts, who lived in a retirement home in Ludlow, and loved the story of her driving into the school only to see a boy walking down the carriage drive, clearly on his way out. She asked what he was doing. He replied that he was running away, to which she said, with no nonsense, 'Well, you'd better go and get your coat, then.' They both went back into school.

Derek Henderson was encouraged to visit – and, pleasingly, did so for the fortieth anniversary of the school – having been justifiably offended when once he had popped in unannounced and the Head at the time had not made the effort to greet or meet him. So many Prep Schools started their lives with one or two founding families often bequeathing their schools to charitable trusts. Heritage is important.

The recruitment of a new Head had followed a rather rapid succession of incumbents. After the retirement of one much-respected Head there was a hiatus; an unsuccessful appointment. The school was again in interim, with the Deputy temporarily the Acting Head. This did not seem to deter applications from a range of good candidates, all married with appropriate curricula vitae, coming from senior positions in good schools. With realistic expectations of success I may have felt less pressure, thereby giving a more natural, human response at interview. Once again, I recall little of the two-stage, thorough recruitment procedure, interviews and presentations, but was over the moon when the Chair called me to offer the job, which I accepted with surprise, gratitude and anticipation.

The word naïve springs to mind again – or perhaps a smidge of desperation in both wanting and needing the job. I was aware of pressure on pupil numbers, some families having fled the school and the leadership turbulence, with consequent financial implications. Local Prep School competition was strong under good, stable leadership. I did not, however, look at the accounts, something that should be done as a matter of course when applying for a Headship. The school was in deficit – not desperately so but worryingly enough. To add to the strain in my first term, the main building boiler gasped its last breath, having been terminally unwell for quite some time. £80,000 had to be found. Through the disruption of the preceding years, the governing board had reconfigured with new members joining; it was a powerful, supportive group. A number put their hands in their pockets and loaned the school £10,000 each; a loan for which, to my knowledge, repayment was never sought.

The Acting Head did not want the post permanently but did, however, wish to see out the year she had given the school before stepping back into her previous role. On a personal basis, this was a potential concern – I needed to work for my own wellbeing but also financially. It did however present a golden opportunity to the benefit of all parties. Moor Park had had no consistent leadership for three years. The previous Chair of Governors had resigned; the board reconfigured and strengthened. What was the strategic direction? Pupil numbers – especially boarding – had declined. Should Moor Park become a day school? Where did the board sit with the founding Catholicity of the school, where the Catholic population was only approximately 33%, and with another, popular, traditional Catholic Prep School not so many miles away?

By mutual agreement the board appointed me in what might be described as a consultancy role for the rest of the academic year. The appointment of a Head and succession is not like the 'real' commercial world where, often, the desk is cleared within days for a spell of gardening leave and then starting in the new position – probably with all sorts of confidentiality clauses. Headships are normally advertised two terms to a year in advance, with a notice period generally of two full terms. Once the new Head has been appointed there can be a rather stagnant interregnum with no-one quite knowing where they are: incoming and outgoing Head, staff, parents, children. The outgoing Head does not wish to make any significant changes which might not be to the liking of the new appointee. The incoming Head is usually in another full-time position, with little capacity to gain some familiarity with the new school.

This situation was different and I began a weekly commute from Devon to Shropshire, staying in the now-vacant Head's apartment on the first floor of the main building. Although I camped in only one room with a bed and desk, this was undeniably a grand apartment, which had been the province of the Head for many years: wainscoting; large rooms; tall, wide sash windows (most of which needing refurbishment). The bathroom had the most enormous bath with lead pipework, views to the lake in the south and distant hills to the east. The loo is better described as a throne.

Within the grounds, starting life as the original mansion stables, was Clock House. This was the girls' boarding house, with the Houseparents occupying a flat on the ground floor. There was a range of dormitories (with too many empty beds) and a large social space that appeared to be a later addition to the original building. The boy boarders inhabited a wing and the second floor of the main building – again under-occupied.

One of the beauties of South Shropshire and very nearby Herefordshire is the sparse population – relative to the busy, more densely packed south-east of England. There is a sense of space, of peace, of a genteel, slower pace of life. There are no motorways in South Shropshire. Tractors tow trailers generally full of spuds, often determining traffic and journey times. Driving from London or Birmingham or via the M5, there is a tangible slowing on leaving the motorway, both literally and emotionally. While an idyllic place to live, pupil recruitment would always be a challenge. At the time, though, there was a gentle increase in population (and wealth) as families fled the hectic pace of the south-east, some part-commuting several days a week. They were drawn by the countryside, the way of life, reasonably priced country properties and Ludlow itself. This was an opportunity.

Two terms were spent getting to know the community and I had individual meetings with all staff. It was a privilege and enormous advantage to have this time as there is a risk when starting a second Headship. Although rare, second

Headships can go wrong with new appointees thinking they know the ropes, which can inflate confidence, giving a gentle lull of security. I am aware of one such Headship, which came to a rather sudden end when I was told the new Head had become rather too close to the parent body. One body in particular, that is.

Every job, every school has a different culture, the tests and trials defined by context and culture. The luxury of this time and the opportunity of individual meetings would pay dividends. A devout loyalty to the school was quickly apparent, with many colleagues having been at the school for some years. While my 'consultancy' role was not operational and I was determined to keep a respectful distance from everyday life, I could feel there was something special about the place – a happy, purposeful, caring, contagious energy.

There was frequent contact with governors when I reported back on my early thoughts and findings. Finances were a real concern although pupil numbers had stabilised with the Acting Head doing a good job with prospective parents. A big question hung over boarding: why operate two separate boarding houses and two sets of boarding staff with many beds lying empty? Market changes indicated a gentle decline in numbers of young boarders nationally, it was unlikely we would ever reach the full, current capacity again.

I recommended closing Clock House and moving the girl boarders to the north wing of the main building. Houseparents would occupy the Head's flat in the main building, with the indomitable girls' matron living in the girls' wing. Part of Clock House would become the Head's accommodation. Here I must confess to an element of self-interest. While it has been a tradition for a boarding Prep School Head to live in or attached to the main house, times have changed. In the twenty-first century especially, the job has become so immersive that some space and distance, no matter how slight, will mean a job better done. In the rest of Clock House, I recommended we opened a day nursery to secure even younger children who might rise through the Pre-Prep and Prep.

This was a major change to the structure of the school, controversial to some, but it could be achieved with relatively limited capital expenditure. It was a vote of confidence for sustaining boarding but at realistic, achievable levels; it was a true co-educational model with one boarding community. There were, however, key staff to consider – notably those already involved in boarding. The girls' Houseparents had been at Moor Park many years, through its boarding heyday when the dormitories were full and girls' boarding much in demand – which was no longer the case. As expected, they were not enamoured of the plans, choosing to leave and not very gracefully. Meanwhile a husband-and-wife teaching team, both with considerable experience and the respect of parents, agreed to move into the Head's flat as Houseparents. While that may all seem very matter of fact, the story told concisely, it wasn't. Difficult decisions will have a ripple effect, especially where personnel, their families, lives and living are affected. These early changes were, however, necessary and urgent if the school was to turn round its fortunes – indeed, to survive.

Over that summer holiday, the building and refurbishment works were carried out. The new Houseparents moved into the grand accommodation in the main house – formerly the Head's accommodation. The north wing of the mansion was prepared for the girl boarders moving from Clock House, where works began on the new Nursery (nicely named 'Tick Tock' by the Acting Head). Part of the building was sectioned off for my accommodation, though the bedrooms remained very much like the dormitories as they had been in a previous existence. The removal lorry travelling from Devon broke down on the M5, delaying occupation of my new home, but I was excited to be moving and preparing for the start of the new term. The next chapter in my career.

A FRESH START

Moor Park had many traditions, one of which was called 'Chapter', an early morning staff meeting before everyone dispersed to their busy days. It was an opportunity for notices and information relating to the day. It also reinforced pastoral care with, for example, a form teacher having heard from a parent or having a concern about a child, and disseminating the relevant information to those present. Of course not everybody could attend as there were boarders to look after or duties around the school as day children arrived. Written minutes were taken and kept in the common room, which everyone was meant to read – and generally did.

One day the kitchen reported that an enormous, catering slab of cheddar had gone missing. This followed a number of smaller disappearances. I raised the matter verbally at Chapter and then put a notice on the common room board. To me it was really quite simple and inoffensive: things going missing from the kitchen, which needed to stop. The principle being obvious to me, I did not expect anyone to be offended, yet one colleague was.

She came stomping into the study, visibly angry and out of character, objecting to the notice. I asked if she was responsible or if she knew who might be, the answer to both being 'no'. I then questioned why she had taken such offence, asking if I could or should have taken another course of action. The matter seems insignificant in writing about it today but the point I try to make is what can sometimes seem the simplest action or decision may have unanticipated consequences, no matter how thorough the forethought – one of the joys of Headship.

Another debate which emerged through Chapter was 'discipline' – that old chestnut! Every school will have a discipline policy yet every teacher will have his or her own personal standards and levels of what is – or is not – acceptable. One person will object to an untucked shirt while another won't even notice. Some cannot or will not distinguish between the formal and informal. Or there are those teachers who court popularity with the children and are reluctant to tell off or sanction. There are those who are too quick to shout – which is normally ineffective unless used rarely and in contrast to the individual's customary demeanour. Some will be quick to devolve responsibility and refer the child upwards to a more senior member of staff.

One colleague wished 'offence A' to lead to 'consequence B' using the escalating scale of sanctions – a formulaic response. Instances of individual children's behaviour were discussed, with the consensus emerging that everything is predicated upon context. A child whose misdemeanour is rare and out of character does not warrant a serious punishment, while another, repeating miscreant may have to escalate through sanctions, getting parents involved where needed. A major proviso, however: the cause of the behaviour, possibly the wellbeing, mental health or cognitive profile or family background, must be taken into account.

With regard to the formulaic colleague, we reminded ourselves of the Benedictine principle of forgiveness and, if matters came to the top, the Head's study should always be the last bastion of clemency. The words attributed to the writer Henry James by his nephew say it all: 'Three things in human life are important: the first is to be kind; the second is to be kind; and the third is to be kind.'

A boarding Prep School needs a dog. A rural Prep School needs a dog. Perhaps every school needs a dog? I morphed into the stereotype with the arrival of Ben, the black Lab. Never having had a dog before, there was a little apprehension. Would I know how to take care of him; would we bond? He was two and a half years old, having come from a family with young children. Their work was taking them away from home for most of the day and they rightly felt this was verging on cruel for the dog, who needed company. What better place than a school?

Every day began with a walk around the perimeter of the estate – winter, summer, rain, snow or shine – after which Ben would join me in the Study. He was incredibly compliant, well-behaved and a brilliant companion. One day I had some important visitors who I would show round the school and who would then join me for a sandwich lunch in the Study. In our absence the chef brought up the laden plates of sandwiches, leaving them, covered, on the low coffee table. We returned to the Study – the door closed – and their astonishment was evident when we opened it to find Ben lying on his bed in the corner. The sandwiches were untouched.

A core strand of pupil welfare and safeguarding is encouraging children to talk; to voice their feelings, concerns or fears. In asking children who they might talk to when they have a worry, it won't take long before one mentions a dog. The child can expound in safety for, very often, it is the recounting, the offloading, rather than the response that is beneficial. We, as adults, are too eager to try and fix; the dog will not answer back, instruct or try to take control.

There was a girl in Year 6 – a weekly boarder. We'll call her Mary. Making friends did not come naturally to Mary; she was reticent, shy and neuro-diverse with an unstable family history. She and Ben formed an immediate attachment. At the beginning of every break Mary would appear at the door, when Ben would leap from his bed, grabbing his lead softly in his jaws, sitting at her feet in anticipation. The lead wasn't really required for he could roam safely unleashed in the company of children within the grounds, a threat to nobody. Other children would join Ben and Mary as they wandered, recognising her privilege in having responsibility for Ben. Thus her friendships and confidence grew.

The things which generally bring us into teaching are passion for the subject taught, wishing to impart that passion and knowledge, to nurture ways – and a love – of learning, to play a central role in the personal development of children or young people. It is ironic, therefore, that the higher one careers up the ladder, the less contact time one has with children. Influence is felt in what might be seen as a loftier way, however – defining the mission, finding ways of delivering or disseminating that vision and creating a culture. The role of a Prep School teacher is often varied: general subjects, class teacher, subject specialist, form teacher, houseparent or tutor, sports coach and so on. Pupils seeing teachers in these different aspects is beneficial as it tends to strengthen that all-important pupil-teacher rapport. The science teacher is a very different person out of the lab and on the sports field.

The role of a Prep School Head is similarly diverse: from governors and strategy to finance and marketing, to inspection and regulation, to mundane operational matters and decision-making. Emails, meetings with parents, paperwork and documentation are all-prevailing, drawing the Head away from contact with children. I believe it is important for the Head, as the lead professional, to teach and be seen to teach.

At Moor Park, for a time I taught the scholarship class English, a throwback to my early career. I loved the challenge of Senior School scholarship papers – those of the most selective schools – engaging with very bright boys and girls. This wasn't so much conventional English teaching for Year 8 pupils; it was and is complex literary criticism along with discursive essay writing technique. All too often, however, I found myself drawn away, missing important lessons, seeing prospective and current parents, meetings over-running: the hurly burly of school life.

The solution, regrettable though it was, had to be finding another subject or lesson which would have a less detrimental impact on the pupils' learning if and when I was pulled away or delayed. Offering 'cover' for an absent colleague was an effective way of seeing different classes, or popping into someone's class saying you would take it, giving them the gift of time.

The religious, spiritual life and chapel were a central part of Moor Park – as one might expect in a school of Catholic foundation. There were some families in the school who chose it specifically for its Catholic ethos and practice. There were some who chose it for the Benedictine principles and ethos. There were some who chose it because they were impressed by results, Senior School destinations or sport; or, of equal importance, they just liked the atmosphere. The Catholic question: how to reconcile all of the above and attract families to fill the school? Trying to please all the people all the time, being everything to everyone, is a futile pursuit.

My personal approach was 'lightness of touch' from the pastoral, spiritual and religious standpoints. I had heard too many priests who, in their strength of faith and adherence to every Catholic principle as laid down by the Pope, put young people off belief, the faith and attending church. The Moor Park chapel was in what must once have been the ballroom and was the first port of call with prospective parents. Always impressed by the grandeur, they would then be subjected to a tentative question about faith and, specifically, Catholicism. The tailored response depended on their answer. Cynical? I'd like to think not. My job was to fill the school and so long as the religious life of the school continued, faithful and undiluted, my conscience was clear.

Through practice and experience I began to realise even the most superficial of connections with prospective parents – perhaps a mutual acquaintance or something more profound, such as Catholicism in this instance, could determine whether they signed up or not. In a small Prep School every prospective parent, every tour, every registration matters, and it is often simply the personal, human engagement between the parents and Head.

Not long after I started at Moor Park, Ludlow was to become the first British town to join Cittaslow – the 'slow food' movement founded in Tuscany. This was an equal and opposite reaction to fast food, promoting the use of local produce and ingredients. On Ludlow's inauguration to the group, the Cittaslow committee was to visit the area and we offered to host their gathering in the large Henderson Hall. In my welcoming words I drew the audience's attention to a sign they had passed on the drive: 'Slow Children'. While I emphasised this was not a reflection on the pupil population, it did seem entirely right that a school that believed in and promoted fundamental human values – Catholic, Christian, of any faith or none – should be part of the Ludlow community and slow movement.

The house in Devon was sold and the children had moved with their mother to a village near Sheffield. I bought a little cottage in Tideswell in the Peak District, which was to be my retreat for time with the children – and what a wonderful part of the world it is. Amongst the many attractions, one feature of the area is disused railway lines which have been converted into cycle tracks, especially appealing for young children as the incline is never too great. We would drive to a former station and hire bikes, Ben in tow, stopping for a picnic in a spot where the views took in the spectacular landscape.

There was an abundance of beautiful walks for Ben: hills and streams. The children loved it. Very close to the house was a trout stream with a footpath running alongside, approached via a former water mill. Ben would happily swim and fetch sticks while the children would wade. On one winter walk, my son stepped onto a floating tree trunk to reach for Ben's stick and, the very moment I uttered words of warning, the log rolled and in he went. Reaching quickly, I grabbed the hood of his favourite camouflage coat and hauled him out of the water. Soaking wet and already beginning to shiver, we began the long march back to the car, water frothing from his wellies, dumping him in a hot shower with blue lips when we eventually got home.

The village was welcoming and a life developed beyond school – despite the challenge of distance and weekend school commitments. With the intensity of running a boarding Prep School and despite the benefit of often very comfortable accommodation, every Head should have a bolthole. Clock House was indeed a homely refuge from the main school building which housed the boarders but you are still there, on site, and everyone knows it. Just a knock at the door or a quick call to see if you will just pop over to resolve a situation or answer a question.

Whether it was the locality, the part of the world, the type of family we attracted, the Catholic ethos or the wonderful atmosphere in the school – or a combination of all – there was a powerful, pervasive sense of community. In most Prep Schools sports matches are well supported by parents and Moor Park was no exception, with the enviable reputation of the best match tea on the circuit. Mass was held fortnightly in the chapel, conducted by Father Jim, the local priest (utterly loyal to the school but whose homilies rose celestially above the heads of his audience), and parents would attend. The school's bonfire night was legendary, choreographed to music, fireworks reflected on the lake.

Drawing on Bedalian principles, we would hold 'Community Project Weekends', clearing brush around the lake in the overgrown woodland, creating an outdoor learning space. The children's garden was given a makeover. Cheap labour, yes, but reinforcing an already strong community; there was no shortage of volunteers, parents, children, families. It may seem glaringly obvious but the combined energy and unified mission – school, parent, child – is immensely powerful. It makes for a better education, enhancing the personal development of the child.

A 'Reflection' written many years later in September 2022 dwelt on the passing of Queen Elizabeth II, made more poignant by the terminal illness of a very special colleague's daughter:

The word 'community' is freely used though I sometimes wonder if we really dwell on its meaning.

On my bookshelf are the twin volumes of the Oxford Shorter English Dictionary. *Look up just one word and the distractions of language make it a surprisingly good read. 'Comity' – courtesy, civility, urbanity; kindly and considerate behaviour towards others. The first definition of 'community': the quality of appertaining to all in common.*

The test of community is never better demonstrated than in the face of challenge. We saw it over the pandemic. We see it now with mourning – both national and within The New Beacon. The school is diverse – some 350 children, each one unique, but of varying background, culture, belief, opinion, talent and size, yet all equal in their value – parts of the whole. It has been powerful, reassuring and affirming this last week to feel the strength and support within our community.

As the nation pauses on Monday [for the funeral of Queen Elizabeth II], I wish you all a most enjoyable weekend. Good luck to our boys in The John Norman Trophy tomorrow and many, many congratulations to our U11 boys who are ISFA regional champions proceeding now to the national competition.

There is no doubt that Headship has become more complicated and invasive over the years. In those early days at Moor Park, it was not uncommon to have a fully free half term, or four to five weeks of safety in the summer. In my experience, that is no longer the case if the multifarious roles and responsibilities of a Prep Head are to be fulfilled effectively. Those little mobile phones, packed with gigabytes, intrude on our lives wherever we are: messages; calls; interminable, incessant emails. Getting off site should be seen as an essential escape valve and not an abrogation of responsibility. The aircraft analogy applies: in the event of a loss of cabin pressure, secure your own oxygen mask first, which will then enable you to help others.

Moor Park was getting back on its feet. Numbers were improving; the Nursery, Tick Tock, was a positive addition; and accordingly, finances were improving. The local reputation was positive, with families recommending us to their friends – those who were local and some moving up from the south-east. I remember telling the apocryphal story at one Speech Day of the Head, at a similar event, saying, 'Last year we stood on the edge of a precipice; this year we have made a giant leap forward.' It was time to consider facility development as well as refurbishing and replacing some of the temporary, prefabricated classrooms, which had become rather permanent.

We were fortunate in having a governor who ran a family business which specialised in maintaining historic buildings – Warwick Castle, for example. With his expertise and time generously given, we drew up a plan for a collection of single-storey, timber-frame buildings all facing inwards to a central, grassy hub. Space to build was not an obstacle on an eighty-five-acre estate. The model for the school was two-class entry, thus each classroom pod had a pair of classrooms connected by a central storage space. Writing in 2024 of buildings that were constructed in the 'noughties', the figure of roughly £80,000 per pod seems unbelievably reasonable.

To support the facility development we embarked on a fundraising venture. The school was not yet fifty years old but there were some influential, wealthy and generous alumni as well as supportive current and past parents. The project was entitled 'Coherence' as the developments, combined, reinforced the aims of the school while also addressing some of the areas which needed closer attention. Donors were unlikely to be excited about an £80,000 classroom block but more likely to be influenced by a new IT suite, a design technology building and better facilities for music.

The school was now making a decent surplus and, with generous donations, all but the music block were completed in my time. Later in my career I benefited from the expert advice of a fundraising development professional but at this time, though I believed wholeheartedly in the projects, I was not good at asking potential donors to open their cheque books. In my view, a fundraising campaign is best led by a trained professional, with the Head giving presentations of the vision to large or small groups. Again, my opinion only, a Prep School Head should only become directly involved with potential donors of high net worth. Parents do not wish to see their Head as a businessman, seeking more than already exorbitant fees; they wish to see someone in whose care their children will be nurtured, supported, challenged – educated, in the broadest sense of the word.

The Head has two key relationships with the Chair of Governors and the Bursar (or equivalently named). Mine was a powerful, multi-skilled, talented, supportive board but the Chair especially had wisdom and experience which proved to be invaluable. A former pupil of Moor Park himself, he had begun his career as a theatre director then successfully undertaken an MBA before moving on to coach senior executives, latterly the top echelons of the burgeoning mobile phone networks. I benefited from that coaching, which not only helped Moor Park but also my growth as a leader, developing skills that would serve me well throughout my later career. He was calm, thoughtful and perceptive – emotionally and practically – with a portfolio of strategies to support and develop leadership. I am sure it was this partnership which was instrumental in bringing Moor Park out of its most challenging time.

The Chair used a model of three concentric circles, a psychological illustration to help understand human behaviour, or at least provide some perspective. The outside, biggest circle was 'interest' – we have, or should have, interest in everything around us. The next, smaller circle is 'influence'. We all have influence over others, generally our families, those closest to us. Heads have considerable influence. The smallest circle is 'control'. It raises an interesting, logical question: what can we actually control? The answer is less than we might think or imagine – particularly in matters relating to others. As a Head, colleagues have to bend to our influence and only in matters of health, safety, regulation and law do we genuinely have control.

I have used this model many times since when trying to give perspective to a challenging situation or personnel matter. One Moor Park parent was a very large potato farmer with multi-million-pound contracts with well-known supermarkets and potato processors (i.e. chip makers). It had been a particularly wet start to the year; roads, rivers and fields were flooded and he had lost most of his submerged crop. When I asked after this, he simply said philosophically, with a grim smile, 'What can I do? I can't control the weather.' I admired his phlegmatic approach.

With his experience of theatre and his coaching role, the Chair had some knowledge and wisdom about speech-writing. As a very young man I had given a best man's speech, muddling the numbered index cards in my nervousness – an embarrassing lesson learnt young. How many Heads have sat through some performance or other thinking throughout, 'What on earth am I going to say at the end?' Informal concerts at the end of the school day clashed with my drama activity. I would turn up for the beginning of the concert, making an end-of-concert speech, 'That was amazing. You all performed so well and with such confidence.'

Those sorts of speeches come almost daily but then there are the big ones: Prizegiving or Speech Day. How to approach that? I have always felt that Prep School parents do not wish to hear interminable speeches about the year's successes or educational philosophy from the Head, a visiting speaker or the Chair of Governors. The Chair's advice was to think of it as the telling of a story or possibly a succession of stories. As teachers, we are all storytellers and performers, but it is a different matter entirely talking to an audience of parents. One of my favourite stories retold at Prizegiving is attributed to Martin Hammond, a former Head of Tonbridge School. When asked what 'type' of boy he wished to have at his school, after a pause, the answer came: 'Orphans.'

Somewhere around 2004, my children moved back down south, settling near Sevenoaks, Kent. A fellow Head, one of the Class of '98, came up trumps: Edward, my younger son, joined St. Michael's School, Otford, a Prep School which was to suit him well. Frankie, meanwhile, had shown her academic potential by winning a place at Tunbridge Wells Girls' Grammar. No mean achievement.

It was their move to the south-east and the difficulty of sustaining real contact with them, along with a feeling that I had another challenge left in me, that ignited the search for another Headship. Ludlow to Sevenoaks did not make for easy weekend contact. While this was the catalyst, I also felt it was time for a fresh pair of eyes at Moor Park, having taken the school as far as I could. Prep Schools are wonderful places and it is easy to become rather too comfortable, which is when a school's dynamism can diminish. I renewed contact with some of the recruitment consultancies and started looking again at the *Times Educational Supplement*. A series of applications followed where I came close but not quite close enough.

In one instance I applied for a prestigious Prep that was unexpectedly looking for a new Head. The incumbent had left suddenly, having been caught in flagrante with a colleague – both male – creating understandable turmoil. As part of the process there was an interview or meeting with some senior pupils where they asked questions of me and I of them. I recall some of their disgruntlement over a new discipline policy, which they felt to be rather too strict and authoritarian. From what they described it seemed to be quite formulaic, which they felt unfair, though I did point out that if they knew the consequences of a particular action then they should avoid that behaviour. They did not dispute the behaviour, just the consequence. Although unsuccessful in this instance I was definitely back on the interview trail.

Moor Park served a number of prestigious Senior Schools, with some girls going to Moreton Hall in North Shropshire and many boys aspiring to Shrewsbury, which at the time was a boys' school. The Registrar, Richard Field, a former Housemaster, was legendary. At those Senior School Fairs which Prep Schools (including Moor Park) offer, with senior staff promoting their schools to parents, Richard's stand had something of the unreconstructed, of the eccentric about it. With a banner behind, the table and surroundings were laden with anything from a cricket bat, a violin, muddy rugby boots, an exercise book and house ties to a pile of prospectuses.

Having been a firm follower of co-education throughout my career, believing in boys and girls growing up together, it was mainly through Richard's influence that I became interested in the concept and benefits of a boys' school. I came to realise growing up together and learning together are two very different things. He was of course persuasive and charming, with a profound belief in his school, where he had been for many years. I also began to see how my former pupils thrived at Shrewsbury.

A MOVE TO SEVENOAKS

One of the most prestigious UK boys' Prep Schools is The New Beacon. It started life as 'The Beacon' in St. John's Road, Sevenoaks, taken over in the late nineteenth century by the Norman family. They negotiated for and bought a rural site on the edge of Sevenoaks, part of the Montreal Estate, designing and building a school which opened in 1900: The New Beacon. The founding family was influential in the early days of IAPS, the development of the Common Entrance exam for independent Senior Schools and the quality control inspection process, which was in its infancy. One of the school's first inspection reports remarked on the inordinate amount of time devoted to Latin and the Classics – a not uncommon phenomenon in the early twentieth century.

When the job was advertised in 2007, the Head had been in post for over thirty years and was a former Chair of IAPS. It was a long, ambitious shot but right in so many different ways: a boys' school, a very different challenge, the perfect location. I applied.

There was a preliminary interview in London before proceeding to the first stage, which involved a tour of the school and a round of interviews, in those days all face-to-face. I was conscious again of my single status but by now had the benefit of seven years' successful leadership behind me. It also felt the right time to move on. Moor Park was addictive, a wonderful place to be, but I felt I had another role in me and believed there was no better time for a change of leadership for the school. The draw of being close to my children was of course very powerful and my Chairman was supportive of applications.

I was delighted to get through the first stage and be invited back for the shortlist interviews to experience one of the most unusual – at times comical – processes extending over two days. On day one we were to check into The Royal Oak hotel, then report to the school for another tour and a series of interviews. Candidates had to teach a lesson. I chose the topic of 'Study Skills', observed by The Head who, other than individual meetings with candidates, was on the periphery of the selection process. The New Beacon had the rightful reputation of being a successful academic school; it would be interesting to gauge the boys' learning habits. I also thought it would be different, which might appeal to the selection panel, and would be an effective free-standing forty minutes not dependent on anything else the class had learnt.

That evening there was a formal dinner with all governors and all candidates. We moved from table to table between courses to be grilled by governors, particularly those who were not part of the selection panel, this being their only opportunity to meet and question candidates. It was an impressive, if somewhat daunting, group: the local MP, partners of city law firms, financiers and a QC who was to become a High Court Judge. The MP told me a conversation had been held about me in the corridors of Westminster with the MP for Ludlow. I recall the food being adequate, the wine very good, and one particular governor who held his notes under the table ensuring he asked all candidates his astute, probing questions.

We were already primed for what was to happen the next morning. We were to check out of The Royal Oak, taking our bags to the school for a further round of interviews. This included the involvement of committee members of the Parents' Association and one question in particular stood out: 'Would you tell us something that would surprise?' A brilliant question over which I initially stumbled but then answered by saying my brother had somehow got tickets for the Rugby World Cup being held in France and would attend every England game.

One of my own favourite questions at interview is 'What makes you mad?' Some people are very slick at interview but may not be so effective in role: questions need to discriminate between the two. This question, although unorthodox, can be revealing – the answer of 'I don't really get mad' does not hold water for me. One purpose of interview is to test, to see how quickly candidates can think on their feet, while also assessing the substance of their answers as well as their emotional intelligence.

In following years, I gave interview practice to those boys who were preparing for Senior School entry and the pre-assessment processes. Done in a year group, calling up volunteer individuals to test them with a question, this was always a lot of fun – their peers enjoying their friends being put on the spot. One boy reduced us all to tears and minutes of laughter by breaking wind as he sat down. He apologised with sincerity and was profoundly embarrassed. We agreed this would not serve him well at the real event.

The end of another gruelling day saw us all convene in the Head's Study. This was *The Apprentice* moment. We were called from the room one by one, our overnight bags stored elsewhere, and went up to the Library, where the panel was assembled. We were told either we were fired or we should check back into The Royal Oak and return the following morning to give a presentation and be subjected to a final interview. I had never come across a process such as this – and never have since. Those who were not selected disappeared, never to be seen again. The remaining three of us had a rather awkward supper that night back at the hotel.

In such processes the presentation usually revolves around how the candidate will build on the successes of the school, develop and propel it into the next era. I cannot recall the precise content of my presentation – the document is long since gone – but I suspect it revolved around pastoral care and personal development. Whatever I said and did throughout the lengthy process, it clearly fell upon receptive ears and I was thrilled to be offered the position.

It was the summer of 2007 – a full year before taking up the appointment in September 2008. There was scant opportunity to visit The New Beacon over that year. Time, distance and a school to run all-prevailing, there was also the process of appointing my successor at Moor Park, which began in the autumn. While delighted at the new position, a fresh challenge and the prospect of once again being closer to my children, when the time eventually came it would be a wrench to leave Moor Park. It was a strange process therefore to see candidates coming for interview, all of whom fitted the bill of leading an independent, rural boarding and day school. While Catholicity was a factor, it was not the defining one – we were selecting the right person with the right pedigree and I agreed with the governors' eventual decision.

The second half of the summer term is always joyful in a Prep School, especially so for the Year 8 children. Those who travel the full length, from Reception upwards, are unlikely to spend so long in one institution over the course of their lives – at least hopefully not. While Common Entrance as a June qualifying exam has been on the decline for a number of years, there is something rather carefree about the time post summer exams with a full, varied leavers' programme. There are ages and stages to education with pupils outgrowing each phase, 13+ in this case, but the same also applying to sixth form and university.

This was similar and poignant for me, too, in the summer of 2008: excitement and anticipation about the next phase of life while also reflecting on seven happy, fulfilling years. The final Speech Day was emotional, a parent commenting after that I had sat down rather suddenly at the end of my speech.

The summer was spent careering down to Kent, moving into a ridiculously large house for a single man. Although the children would have their own bedrooms, there was still plenty of room to fill. I collected the keys and also took occupation of the study, reconfiguring it from my predecessor's arrangement. He had the desk positioned in the bay window, from which his back could be seen (or not) by the passing parental traffic. Remembering the military gentleman's advice and also wishing not to be quite so apparent to all eyes, the desk moved elsewhere. In a further change, the door was pinned open, where I understood it had in the past been closed. Symbolic changes.

The INSET (training) days came round very quickly. With the school having been under the same leadership for decades, there was understandable apprehension and anticipation amongst the staff. After an initial introduction, a bit of background about my career and what I stood for, I divided everyone into small groups, asking them to do a 'SWOT' analysis. Each group was led by a member of the Senior Team, its composition having representation across the age-related sections of the school. While there may be other methods of delving into the ethos, pros and cons of a school, I feel this remains one of the most effective and my new colleagues picked up the challenge – there was healthy, lively debate. There's a story of an inspector passing a member of staff in the corridor and asking, 'What is this school all about?' The teacher replies, 'I don't know, I just teach Latin.' To enrol and involve colleagues, they need to be part of the bigger thinking and, I would regularly give a presentation giving an outline of the school's finances, an assessment of local market forces and emerging trends.

I remember using the expression 'everything is up for grabs' – any aspect of school life, perceived strengths, weaknesses, opportunities or threats could be questioned. One subject came up very quickly and I suspect it related more to the length of the staff week and duties rather than a matter of principle. A question was raised about Senior School (Year 7/8) Chapel, which was held most Fridays at 5pm; not just questioning if this practice was appropriate but was it the right time of the day and week? Having said everything was 'up for grabs', I said I felt such a tradition was an important part of school life and the boys' spiritual education. It would stay.

One aspect of school life I had noticed on a visit the previous year was the queue for lunch. The traditional dining-room, originally table service but now cafeteria, was too small for the number of pupils, with lunch taken on a rota basis, finishing with the oldest boys. The top years sometimes had to queue for more than fifteen minutes before getting served, thereby losing a large portion of their break. This was a rowdy, disorderly affair with big, hungry, understandably impatient boys. It not only delayed their lunch; it impacted on their important free time, respite from a full academic programme, impinging on music lessons, team practices and so on. The daily routine, and especially lunchtime, was identified as a matter for urgent scrutiny. The shape of the day was one of the first changes implemented.

Every school has its curiosities and surprises; there is much to absorb in the early days of a new position. Those things that are familiar and routine to the staff will be entirely unfamiliar to a new Head, who cannot avoid asking questions which must appear trite. I am reminded of Basil saying to Sybil in *Fawlty Towers*, 'Can't we get you on Mastermind, specialist subject the bleeding obvious?' In my first week a boy approached me in the corridor and asked if he could have an 'E'. More than a little concerned and beginning to wonder what sort of place I had come to, I asked for clarification, to discover it was a reward system. Teachers could recommend an E for excellence to be approved and awarded by the Head.

Systems and roles often evolve based on the skills and talents of staff, as well as the addition and ideas of new, incoming colleagues. The senior team held some very able, capable, loyal members. The curiosity was its composition, with two Deputies and one Assistant Head, all, apparently, on an equal footing. There was no direct Deputy who would lead in the Head's absence – the 'fall under a bus' scenario. None of them claimed the position. Neither was there a job specification to clarify. This would need addressing but not until my feet were slightly further under the desk, with better knowledge of my colleagues.

A further surprise arose very early in my tenure, which quickly bubbled up to the surface due a serious pastoral incident between two boys. One alleged that the other had indulged in inappropriate sexual behaviour in the boarding house. Such was the seriousness of the allegation it was regarded as a child protection matter, hence the social services were contacted. Their advice taken, a full investigation followed. The boys in question were interviewed at length and, similarly, other boys who boarded on the same nights. It seemed most likely there had indeed been some inappropriate behaviour. Both sets of parents were contacted. Those of the 'victim' were deeply upset, angry, even questioning if the school had needed to investigate their son's disclosure. The parents of the alleged perpetrator (for want of a better word) were indignant and resistant. They had spoken to their son, who denied everything; they believed him unequivocally.

At this delicate point I asked my PA for a copy of the parent contract. Alarm bells were ringing and both parents just happened to be litigating lawyers. The PA looked a little bewildered for a moment. 'You mean the parent contract regarding fees?' she asked. 'Er, no, the one which sets out full terms and conditions, disciplinary policy, the Head's decision on such matters and so on.' To my dismay, the long and short of it was that no such contract existed – something we put right very soon afterwards, adapting a template policy from the school's lawyers. We did, however, through necessity, take legal advice.

I felt it would be wise for the perpetrator to leave the school and to choose an alternative Senior School out of the immediate area. Sevenoaks has a tight community, rife with gossip and misinformation, on occasion revealed to be scurrilous. There was plenty of chat amongst the parents in the year group and his peers had begun to ostracise him – albeit without any overt animosity. I felt for his parents, the indignity and embarrassment, but they did come round to my way of thinking and I set to finding the right school. Through strong contacts with many boarding Senior Schools built during the years at Moor Park, a place was secured at a very good school and I was pleased to hear later that he had been one of the top performers at Common Entrance.

PARENTS & PARTNERSHIP

The thin contractual ice I had found myself crawling over, trying to diffuse the weight and load, raised consciousness of parental support (or not) for the school or Head in disciplinary matters. Once upon a time, rightly or wrongly, if a child came home from school having been in trouble, or if the school got in direct contact themselves, there would be no question: trouble at school; trouble at home. Winston Churchill said, 'Headmasters [sic] have powers at their disposal with which Prime Ministers have never yet been invested.' I assume he was referring to what might have seemed to be 'absolute' power and he may well have had a contemporaneous point, but that was then. It is absolutely right, today, that any incident is investigated thoroughly – those pupils directly implicated as well as any witnesses questioned – and the Head should be answerable to parents and external authorities.

I am generalising here, but over the years parents have without doubt become more forceful in defence of their children when a misdemeanour is alleged, often without forethought or considering the school's motivation. While there may sometimes be grey areas (the perspectives, perceptions and memories of young people having some variety) and a lack of absolute clarity, is a school really going to rattle a hornets' nest without having confidence in its assertions? In one instance, a furious father came to the study door, kicking away the doorstop in anger. It crashed against the French windows, which somehow stayed intact. His son had been caught live, midst misdemeanour, yet the father was in staunch denial.

John Rae, former Head Master of Westminster, used a lovely expression when talking to new parents, something which I adopted and repeated year on year: 'If you believe only half of the stories which come home from school, we in turn will believe only half the stories which come to school from home.' Or words to that effect. A child comes home resenting the teacher who called him a 'disgusting elephant'. The angry parent phones school, only to discover the boy had been called a 'disruptive element'. We all wish to defend our children, though the knee-jerk defence does not take account of the full circumstance.

The great majority of parents are, however, fully supportive. That triangular relationship between school, pupil and parent makes education work. With colleagues I would sometimes refer to the Pareto principle, the 80:20 rule: 80% of the time is spent on 20% of the parents; in truth, probably less than 20%, nearer 10%. The advice was always to pick up the phone or arrange a meeting in person or, more latterly, virtually. Emails are subject to interpretation no matter how carefully composed; parents will often pick at the bone of contention.

On a number of occasions I found myself the arbiter between parents who could not agree, more often than not on the choice of Senior School: father wants School A; mother prefers School B. The child is of course at the centre of the debate. Which school do I think would suit him better? Both options are achievable. The repeated advice to parents was to do their research, narrow down their list, visit the schools, ask pre-prepared questions. All things being equal, choose the preferred option based on 'feel', atmosphere and instinct. Having gone through this process with some intensity, the parents then asked me to decide.

My suspicion is that something deeper, murkier, lurks beneath this debate where I have been called upon to adjudicate. The decision must be theirs; I can advise but they must reach a compromise and consensus between them.

There are few positives to getting divorced but, with some irony, my own experience has been helpful when supporting parents who are going through the same painful process. The children can be forgotten or even weaponised in the midst of grief and anger, contact and finances the frequent, emotional artillery. More than one conversation has needed firm words: 'How do you think this is for your children? At least you have that one thing in common – whatever your differences, you made them together.'

In Pre-Prep there is that lovely start to the day where

children filter in, happy to see their friends, chatting and getting on with the first task the teacher will have set. In one class the teacher overheard one boy saying to his friend, 'Your daddy had a sleepover with my mummy last night.' Sweet, sweet innocence. The teacher spoke with the Head of Pre-Prep and the matter was brought to me with some urgency. In the case of the hosting, sociable, sleepover mum, separation and divorce proceedings had already begun. With the other family, nothing of the sort – a bolt out of the blue. All hell broke loose. Both mothers, collecting their boys at the end of the day, had an unrestrained shouting match, witnessed by all the other parents as well as the children in the class – including their own. At least two parents contacted me asking for the school's intervention.

Memorable meetings ensued. The sleepover mother was indignant: what did parental matters (affairs) outside of school have anything to do with me? What business was it of mine? She was not receptive to the fact that children and parents had witnessed the shouting match, or indeed to the consequent emotional confusion for her own son, who was already very aware of his parents' separation and the associated antagonism. My priority was the safety and security of all the children, never mind parent decorum. As for the other mother, there began a very painful, public breakdown of her family.

Bruce Grindlay, then Head of Sutton Valence School, wrote an excellent letter to parents of his pupils that hit the national media. He referred to 'overprotective' parents with 'time-consuming and unpleasant repercussions' when a child was sanctioned or a 'behavioural concern raised'. I have known many an occasion where a teacher has not taken disciplinary action fearing the vigour of a parent's response. How does a child learn in such circumstances?

From application and at the very outset, I was conscious of the fact that the parent demographic would be different at The New Beacon. Families at Moor Park on the whole comprised the rural, farming or landed, and 'professionals', a good number having fled the pace of life in the south-east. They were of course ambitious for their children, investing huge amounts on school fees and wanting them to go to good schools – more boarding than day – but they were, on the whole, less stridently competitive.

Many parents at The New Beacon worked in the city: finance, investment, trading, banking, law and insurance. Their world was high-octane. It was not unusual for that to be reflected in their approach to schooling: they were highly ambitious for their children. It was also evident in the Parents' Association quiz nights (see p. 108). The staff team winning was, we thought, reassuring for parents. Competition was strong. One year a parent approached the scoreboard, wiped off her team's score and added a bigger number. Another year a parent had to be ejected for heckling and arguing, somewhat the worse for wear from alcohol.

The parents' association had an AGM at which the Head was invited to speak and then take questions. I was already aware of a plague of tutoring in the Sevenoaks area and chose to raise this in my first address. Neither

I nor the school, historically, approved of tutoring – the curriculum was adequate in itself and calibrated to each child's ability, potential and development.

I recounted to them the tale of a conversation I had with the Head of Judd, one of the most selective Grammar Schools in the area. I had asked him about the biggest challenge he faced in his school, expecting the answer to be funding, staffing, class size – any number of things but tutoring. He told me that boys were coached and tutored within an inch of their lives. On successfully gaining entry to Judd they would find the pace, the expectation, too much. Behavioural and mental health concerns would inevitably follow. At the AGM, a senior colleague was sitting near the back who told me afterwards one parent had leant and whispered to another, 'Who does he think he is, telling us that?'

Everyone is an educational expert because we have all been to school. Some are patronisingly quick to instruct their children's teachers; it is indeed they who are the experts in education. The facts that techniques and practice have thankfully evolved over time, and pastoral care is more enlightened are carelessly neglected. There are few things more frustrating for a teacher than a parent asserting, 'Well, this is how I learnt fractions.' Or, in one instance, a mother saying, 'Well, I was at Oxford and my husband was at Cambridge; why isn't Bertie performing at the top of the class?'

Only with the benefit of experience and many meetings with parents did it dawn on me that it was possible to tell if parents had a bad educational experience themselves. More often than not it would be the father, just looking a little uncomfortable in the Head's study, sometimes defensive, occasionally abrasive, even when the subject matter was an open conversation about the next school. Whatever the motivation for a meeting, trying to find common ground, putting the parent at ease, listening, conceding ground where necessary and admitting when the school has got it wrong all make for better parent relations.

Reflections 30.9.22

I had a very enjoyable meeting with some prospective parents this week when we delved into what The New Beacon is truly about – what is our magic; our secret formula?

The word 'competition' came into the conversation more than once. Though sometimes confused, the words 'attainment' and 'achievement' are not interchangeable. The former relates to a pre-defined standard – clearing 1m in the high jump, reaching a 50% pass mark and so on. Achievement is different, measured only by individual ability, potential, ambition and endeavour. A reticent boy in my class having the growing confidence to put up his hand and answer a question – that is an achievement.

We cannot escape competition: for a place in a team, in a race, for a place at senior school or university – for a job. We do not talk about failure in school – we talk about disappointment. We can rationalise disappointment and find a stronger way forward: was I too ambitious; was the competition just too good; did I not prepare thoroughly?

The most important facet of competition, however,

> *lies within. Children cannot help but compare themselves with others. As they mature, however, they learn to measure their successes against their own ambitions. They learn self-discipline and develop self-determination.*
>
> *And this is where the word 'achieve' is more powerful and personal than 'attain'. Everyone can achieve. Everyone can do well at effort; though we can't always attain or meet our ambitions. In a variation on the oft-quoted words, 'It is better to have tried – and been disappointed – than never to have tried at all.' Therein lies a New Beacon mantra: expect much of children and they will surprise.*

The first year at The New Beacon was something of a baptism of fire. The complicated pastoral, child protection matter was concurrent with a staff disciplinary concern. One colleague, experienced and relatively recently joined, alleged she was being bullied by another more senior colleague. There was email evidence to support her allegation and she had the backing of another senior, long-standing, highly respected colleague who had witnessed encounters between the two. There was also some disrespectful 'form'. She had written a scathing email to her husband reacting to an email from the Head, my predecessor (including vocabulary to shock the ether), carelessly pressing 'reply' as opposed to 'forward'. Sadly, these things will happen in any workplace and we've all pressed the wrong button.

Policy must be followed but the first stage is to try to achieve an amicable resolution. I raised the matter informally with the subject of the complaint. Her aggressively defensive response was immediate. I recall a union was involved from the outset.

New in position, not yet knowing the characters and dynamics of the common room, having a very different leadership style from my predecessor and not yet having formed a firm rapport with the Chair of Governors, I felt somewhat vulnerable. The school's legal advisors became involved, as did those of the defendant. The matter was taken to an employment tribunal, by which time she had secured another position and chosen to leave the school. To my principled regret but probably pragmatically, as is so often the case in these situations (governors wary of negative media attention), a financial settlement was agreed. As far as TNB was concerned, the matter ended there, leaving the defendant free to continue with similar behaviours in other schools. I understand she did.

Personnel matters are the most challenging, whether they be interactions within the common room or performance-related. Interactions between colleagues are difficult to substantiate, evidence in short supply; one word against another, they are subjective. Performance, too, requires evidence. Lesson observations, appraisal, performance management meetings, all with written reports, are standard fare. Measurable targets follow, as needed, with a clearly defined timeframe. Underperformance in whatever form cannot be allowed to continue without intervention. Experience brings one to take legal advice at an early stage – instinct should tell there is a storm brewing. It may seem easier to take a passive approach in the hope that time will bring improvement but this is a risk; decisive, early intervention will bring short-term anxiety but with longer-term benefits and the likelihood of school improvement.

The next personal crisis was an anonymous letter sent to the Chair of Governors alleging all sorts of spurious things about my leadership. Within the school there had been a similar instance some years previously. A vitriolic, anonymous letter had been sent to the Head about an altogether different, senior member of staff. The Head had even gone so far as having all staff produce a sample of handwriting with a graphologist trying to make a comparison to identify the perpetrator.

All to no avail. The writer was never uncovered and, in this instance, there was more than a suspicion of someone wishing to continue sharing the venom. The Chair of Governors chose to call in a few members of the senior team to see if there was any substance to the anonymous allegations and, thankfully, I had their support. My view at the time – and since – is no credence should be given to someone who has not the courage to identify themselves (albeit in confidence) and provide substance to their allegations.

It wasn't all bad. Post appointment but before joining The New Beacon, the Chapel Choir Director approached me on one visit to the school. He asked if I would be supportive of a Chapel Choir tour to Venice and, if so, would I come along to see the choir for myself? As decisions go, this was an easy one: yes to both, without hesitation. The first half of my first term done, I found myself at Gatwick

Airport at some ungodly hour with twenty-five choristers and a number of staff. How wonderful to be on a school trip with no direct responsibility for the itinerary or first-hand pupil supervision – though I was permitted to bring my younger son, who would always need supervision.

The private airport waterbus took us to the Ferrovia stop by the railway station and then a short walk to our hotel. We later discovered this was the very same hotel Michael Palin had stayed in when filming *Around the World in Eighty Days*. He was equally amazed by an establishment which had the pretensions of being a hotel; a comfortable, hospitable place to stay.

As with many hotels in Venice, it did feel rather crammed in among neighbouring buildings, but we were also equally crammed into our rather stale rooms. I remember ours having a large hole in the traditional Venetian marble flooring, which my son found most amusing. There was a postage stamp of an outdoor space where staff convened for a drink in the evening – shocked to be berated by some jet-lagged Australians for making too much noise one night.

On the staff team was the delightful Chapel Choir Director, Andrew Snowdon, as well as the aforementioned member of staff about whom there had been an allegation of bullying, and of course, the organist, Lucy Faulkner. Having sung in choirs as a child and also having enjoyed choirs in the various schools where I had worked, I quickly began to realise this was something quite different. There was a quality and ambition not previously encountered in the many schools where I had worked. My experience of choirs and chapel choirs in co-educational schools was the predominance of girls, particularly in senior choirs in Years 7 and 8. Adolescent boys begin to lose confidence in their breaking voices, fearing embarrassment in front of the girls, whereas in a boys' school, there is genuinely less inhibition. Boys auditioned for the chapel choir and there was no shortage of applicants.

On the tour schedule was a concert in The Redentore, Giudecca, with the choir also accompanying Mass in St. Mark's Basilica. Andrew, crowning himself on a buttress in the crypt of St. Mark's awaiting the mass, was careless in his expletive, much to the amusement of the boys. These were to be lifelong, extraordinary experiences for the boys, for all who participated and the relatives who joined us.

It was the first true moment of camaraderie I had felt since joining The New Beacon, no doubt aided by being away from school with a small group of boys and staff, all united in mission. Andrew was great company with an easy laugh, which echoed around the acoustic of the wonderful buildings where they rehearsed. Lucy was – and is – an exceptional organist, having been organ scholar at Jesus College, Oxford, and was also delightful company. It is relatively rare in life – arguably exceptional – to feel a profound connection with another human being, which is exactly what seemed to be happening. On return from the tour, retiring to the peace and safety of North Norfolk, the rest of half term was spent agonising over the potential joys (and risks) of initiating something which I felt could be special.

In short, the risk was to be taken, such opportunities

being few and far between in a world where happiness is not always easily found. Lucy and I began to see each other socially, discreetly, away from school, becoming engaged that December. The staff meeting announcing the engagement early in the Spring Term was a moment to treasure. Astonished faces.

In the following years, biennially, the chapel choir toured Dubrovnik, Rome and Venice. Printed in small font tucked on a corner of each programme could be found the adopted motto of the Choir of St. George's Chapel, The New Beacon, '*Quid fortasse erret*' – 'What could possibly go wrong?' In the most recent tour to Dubrovnik the boys were depositing their baggage through the EasyJet automated check-in when one of my group said he thought he'd left his passport on the top of his suitcase as it disappeared into the entrails of Gatwick. Indeed he had, and the airport staff were successful and brilliant in tracking it down. Dubrovnik was a favourite tour venue, accompanying Mass and performing a concert in the cathedral. The boys enjoyed the pedestrian freedom of the walled city, the boat trip to the island of Lokrum and the still-warm October sea for swimming.

Singing in St. Peter's Basilica, The Vatican, will be a lifelong memory for all those who were there and, in a break away from Catholic protocol, I was given the extraordinary honour of reading the Gospel. Just walking the streets of Rome is fascinating in its own right, pointing out the sights to the boys, who were under instruction to keep their mobile phones in their pockets and who were, on the whole, interested. For Lucy, on one tour, the pressure of playing in St. Peter's was enhanced by the cleric, who had mislaid the key to the organ keyboard, opening it only two minutes before the service.

A less savoury memory was an outbreak of Norovirus on one tour of Rome. First, a single poor boy was sick and matron had to remain at the hotel with him. Then another boy, then another, went down with the horrible sickness bug. It was the last day of the tour when we took the coach to the centre of Rome to meet with families who would take their boys to lunch. As we got off the coach one boy was violently ill right next to me – undoubtedly better off the coach than in. Staff then had a lovely opportunity for lunch and a break before gathering again, meeting the boys and going to the airport.

When we arrived at Fiumicino Airport and having passed through security, I became aware of feeling rather odd. By the time we boarded the aircraft I felt very unwell. A kind parent, seeing my discomfort, swapped seats so my delicate situation was less apparent to the boys. I learnt that day of the aerosol properties of sickness, suffering the embarrassment of being wheeled through Gatwick when we landed.

In a later return visit to Venice, I remember the celebration dinner after the final concert – an event which became something of a celebrity moment for the boys as we were joined by our 'groupies' – parents and relatives revelling in the tour. Our Venetian restaurant hosted not just the tour group but also more than eighty groupies, all eating well and drinking vats of wine. The atmosphere, the support for the boys and staff, for a fantastic tour, was palpable. At the end of the evening I went to pay the school (not parent) bill and was shocked to see the maitre d' charging us for the staff wine, which by prior agreement had been included. Although I had no Italian, a dispute followed where I pointed out they had benefited from a highly profitable evening with all the custom – eighty-plus adults, eating and drinking with little restraint, who had accompanied us. To my surprise and pleasure he just screwed up the bill, vented (probably in some offensive way) and let us go.

Reflections 23.9.22

As the evenings begin to draw in it is a warming thought to cast our minds back to the wonderful NBPA [parents' association] fete on that glorious summer afternoon. The NBPA does a grand job for the school – I am grateful for their commitment and that of the class reps.

One topic which came up before their meeting this week was music. The school has a long, strong musical tradition – in part, I believe, due to being a boys' school. Musicians regularly win scholarships to their next schools and three former pupils are currently organ scholars at Oxford/Cambridge colleges.

But what of the value of music education? From the very earliest years, our boys sing – it is normal to sing. Ella Fitzgerald: 'the only thing better than singing is more singing'. The chapel choir is bulging at the seams with new volunteers seemingly every day and many of them are travelling to Dubrovnik at half term to accompany Mass in the cathedral and perform a concert.

Instrumental music is thriving: 16 peripatetic

teachers giving over 300 individual instrument and vocal lessons weekly with 18 ensembles from Y2 upwards. Music is best made together. Informal concerts give boys the opportunity to build confidence in performance while bigger events and concerts bring boys together in ensembles and orchestras with the lateral lesson and benefit of working together as a team.

While music has its own intrinsic value it is also a vital part of a holistic education, stimulating the whole brain, a central element of New Beacon life. Further down this page you will find a link to a document which outlines everything musical on offer at The New Beacon. The biographies of the staff, 'resident' and peripatetic, make impressive reading.

As an anecdote, some years ago there was a typo on the signing-in book for the music block. It was labelled the 'singing in' book. Or was it indeed a typo?

'Music is a moral law. It gives soul to the universe, wings to the mind, flight to the imagination, and charm and gaiety to life and to everything.' *Plato*

HIERARCHY

With the angle of my desk changed and very aware of the risks of moving too far, too fast, I knew the senior team did have to be reconfigured in that first year. This was an experienced group of people, all of whom had been at the school for many years – a delicate tread would be needed. There was one outstanding candidate for Deputy, who was the glaringly obvious choice. She baulked at the opportunity, having concerns about how the others might feel, but on reflection and possibly with some persuasion agreed to be a proper Deputy, standing above the others in seniority. Whether this move had something to do with the anonymous letter and injured feelings I will never know, but there was now a Senior Management Team with clearly defined responsibilities.

Job titles, labels and hierarchy give rise to caution. It is easy for teachers and even middle management to throw stones at leadership teams. The SMT (Senior Management Team) was essentially an operational group dealing with matters of policy, yes, but very much running the day-today life of the school. Mindful of the sensitivities within that group and rather than create a Senior Leadership Team, I formed the 'Strategy Group', which comprised the Deputy, School Business Manager and one colleague who, coincidentally, had been one of the Class of '98, she and her husband having run another Prep School together. This was an able, supportive group that operated at strategic level, looking at ethos, marketing and development in all its forms: academic, pastoral, facility and so on. A leadership and management structure was now in place.

I have always had enormous respect – if not admiration – for those who teach the youngest in our schools. In all sincerity, I couldn't do it. In the SMT was the Head of Junior School and Pre-Prep – a big role indeed. My predecessor had appointed, separately, a Head of Pre-Prep, a teacher of considerable experience. A problem did however emerge as these two sections were in different buildings and something of a rift developed, each inclining towards their own separate entity – slowly, gently but perceptibly. It was understandable for the Head of Junior School to feel a little undermined.

Binding the junior and senior ends of a Prep School is not an unfamiliar problem, with the junior end feeling that the senior end takes precedence and priority; the senior end, however, feeling their day is longer with duties often beyond 6pm, see those colleagues working with the younger years leaving school considerably earlier. A few, the more militant perhaps, might even add up the minutes of contact time and compare.

When I worked in the Prep attached to a Senior

School, I remember a Head of Department referring to the Prep teachers as 'sticklebrickers'; there seems to be an unwarranted hierarchy of respect based on the age of the children or young people taught. The Head of Junior School and Pre-Prep, highly regarded by parents, chose to leave and I was fortunate in having the ideal candidate already on the staff for an internal appointment, providing continuity and stability.

And so to the other key figure for the Head: the Bursar, or Business Manager or Director of Finance and Operations or Chief Financial Officer. Titles and roles have evolved and grown over the years. Talking to fellow Heads, I have heard many horror stories of personality clashes and differences of ideology with their Bursars. The two roles require very different skills, and often personalities, but they need to be complementary and collaborative. While the Head must have good business sense as well as an understanding of budgeting and accounting, the role is primarily outward and people-facing. The Bursar is often found in some remote eyrie in front of a bank of computer screens – or at least that is the stereotype – with the word 'no' seeping down the corridor. Many Bursars come from a business background, banking or accounting and, even today, from the military. The training, structure and systems of the armed forces lend themselves well to managing the business side of a school, though the style can sometimes seem rather incongruous.

My impression of many people in this role – and I have been very fortunate – is they can be baffled and bemused by the lack of business sense in teachers. A Bursar at one school where I worked would close all academic departmental budgets in May, saying if it wasn't spent by that stage, it wasn't needed. He had seen many teachers empty their budgets late in the summer term for fear of having it reduced the following academic year, which of course runs counter to business planning. In my view Bursars should be facilitators – within reason. There will be vision, strategy and a development plan, all costed, but there will also be contingency, and it is not unknown for a Head to seek to plunder that secret coffer which every good Bursar should keep. Prep Schools particularly, being smaller than many Senior Schools, require very careful financial management – the bottom line easily and quickly affected by just a small fluctuation in pupil numbers. The best Bursars know how to say 'no' nicely.

I had my predecessor to thank for taking the bold step of stopping Saturday morning school a year or two prior to my arrival. For the first time in my career, I was working in a weekly boarding school with Saturdays free of the usual routine. That said, there were many matches well supported by parents. Watching good school sport is a pleasure, not a burden, and a convenient opportunity to chat with parents on the touchline – not just for visibility but also learning much about individual boys and any underground rumblings about the school.

The full boarding days of TNB were long gone and fourteen beds were only occupied Monday to Thursday inclusive. For some it was weekly boarding, arriving Monday morning and leaving Friday evening. For others there was the option of 'part boarding', a model that was different to flexi-boarding and which tempted the occasional sleepover – a convenience for parents but just fun for the boys staying with their friends, unable to resist the temptation of chatting into the wee hours of the night. The structure and routine of boarding is important if it is to fulfil the aim of developing independence and nurturing personal responsibility. 'Occasionals' would disrupt that structure while those who boarded regularly, if only for one night a week, would learn the routine.

The school day ended at 4.30pm for the older boys, with an optional activity programme to 5.30. Those who boarded would come upstairs for a meeting with the Housemaster where the plan for the evening would be discussed and decided, for example prep (homework) first, before supper, or fun first – the sports hall, astro or swimming pool – and then prep after supper. The boys had a voice in planning their evening, although to say it was a democracy would be going too far.

While on the subject of democracy, some years later a Year 6 boy came to see me one day saying he disagreed with chapel. He no longer wished to attend and suggested the same right should be extended to any boy. I was proud of the school having a culture where a young boy felt able to raise the matter with me. He was an international pupil and we discussed how integrated he felt in the school; had he ever been on the receiving end of a racist comment from another boy? I was pleased, reassured, to hear he had not. We talked about other boys in the school referring to a frequent theme in assemblies and chapel which was 'respecting difference'. Conveniently, coincidentally and ironically, the very same theme had been part of that week's chapel assembly, when he must have been listening because, when asked, he remembered. I told him of a boy, a practising Muslim, who had left the previous year who still attended chapel – indeed never even questioned attendance – because he respected the principles of the school and its Christian foundation. I finished by saying he had a voice and was right to raise any question, but the school was not a democracy and he would continue to attend chapel.

So, to the mission: what was I to bring to TNB? It had a reputation of the posh school at the top of the hill, with more than a hint of superiority accompanied by a small helping of arrogance. There is a brilliant prayer originating from Kenya that I have used in assemblies and taken from the Downside prayer book:

'From the cowardice which dares not face new truth; from the laziness that is contented with half truth; from the arrogance which thinks it knows all truth, good Lord, deliver us.'

Working in the independent sector of education especially, it is our duty as teachers, educators and influencers to remind the pupils of their good fortune. Their privilege should never be taken for granted. I cannot abide arrogance, finding it deeply unattractive. In revising the school's mission statement a year or two later, aspirational words were added to say we hoped to develop young men who were confident but not arrogant – a statement often noted and commented on by prospective parents. Reputations can be undeserved, outliving their time, and the reality of change as the behaviour of a few can unfairly taint an entire organisation. An Australian parent told me of 'tall poppy syndrome', which refers to those who criticise high-achieving people or organisations. TNB sent many children to highly selective schools, therefore, in the view or words of some, it should be scythed like the tall poppy.

The nineteenth-century French novelist, Gustave Flaubert, wrote, 'There is no truth. There is only perception.' I have raised this precept with the Year 8 scholars, having an entertaining, interesting and intelligent discussion to follow. The truth is that some boys at the school did have a sense of entitlement, as is the case in many independent schools. My challenge was to reduce that number, to change behaviour as well as perception. I recall some research carried out by Cambridge University – at least twenty years ago – which measured and ranked influences on children's social and emotional development. Unsurprisingly the strongest influence was parents and home. Disturbingly, even back then the media was the second strongest influence. Schools got only the bronze medal.

A slightly less erudite quote from the character Harry Bosch, a California detective, created by Michael Connelly: 'Everybody counts or nobody counts.' Many parents chose TNB as primarily an academic school from which their boys might progress to academically selective Senior Schools, notably Tonbridge and Sevenoaks, both on our doorstep. While their expectations, their aspirations, may on occasion have exceeded what was achievable, there was a widely held perception that TNB catered only for the brightest and the most resilient.

My initial impressions were of grains of truth in this reputation. Quite rightly non-selective on entry, while the gene pool was strong, we did have children with a range of ability as well as those with learning difficulties. Each child deserved the same care, attention and tailored opportunities. Running alongside this outdated reputation was the illogical conclusion that TNB must be a 'pushy hothouse' to achieve the results it did, with so many boys successfully gaining entry to highly selective schools.

There are few things more difficult than changing human behaviour – unless an individual chooses to change. A prosaic example: parents' driving and parking on the school site. Despite repeated implorations in letters and emails regarding the safety and consideration of others, some would persist in parking unsafely or inconsiderately. The big test here was culture change and where there is culture change, there will always be detractors quick to criticise and destabilise.

Reflections 10.2.23

It's curious how reputations can stick and linger. There are still visitors and prospective parents who ask about the myth of The New Beacon being something of a hothouse. An Australian parent some years ago brought 'tall poppy syndrome' to my attention. Apparently there is now a book: The Joy of Cutting Other People Down. We have had a succession of prospective parents this week and all have commented on the atmosphere in school: happiness, laughter, good manners.

Mythology dispelled.

We heard this week from a former pupil who was at The New Beacon in WW2. Joining the navy he rose to the dizzy heights of Deputy Commander-in-Chief Fleet. Our 'boys' go on to do the most amazing things.

I wonder how many traditions remain from his time here? 'Companies' certainly do – and probably Quarter Plusses, too. In the half term tradition I announced the (current) leaders this morning (well done, Nelson!) and later this term we have the Company Music competition, a very special annual event. Parents sometimes ask about the Head's letter mentioning 'holiday haircuts': a tradition inherited from my predecessor – appearance matters!

Returning to mythology, the truth and essence of the school is that we have a tradition of high expectation – in all the boys undertake; in how we and they are with each other. This week there has been a focus on kindness for it is personal qualities which people often remember first and foremost.

'Expect little of children, they will disappoint; expect much and they will surprise.'

MISSION

Back to careering, the challenge of the first Headship – I would argue any first Headship – was mainly and simply learning to be in charge, the decisions resting on one individual. At Dunhurst, with the support of a Senior School Head and a sensible strategy I felt things had been going well – bar the family situation, of course. In the second Headship, having some understanding of leadership was helpful and the mission was clear: restore stability and confidence following an unstable few years for the school. A wise man told me the second Headship can actually bear more risk, the incumbent believing the job to be already familiar. This, the third Headship, was really quite different – taking over from someone who had been Head for decades, running the school in very much his own way. To me the mission was clear: changing the reality as well as the perception of TNB's culture.

Where the staff were concerned, there was much discussion about pastoral care, the role of the form teacher and the Head of Section: Pre-Prep and Junior, Middle (Y5/6) and Senior (Y7/8) Schools. The younger ones spend most of their time with one teacher, watching and knowing the boys, making observations of changes in behaviour and overall wellbeing much easier. For Year 5 upwards, where boys migrate from room to room, from teacher to teacher, the picture can be much more fragmented. Effective internal communication is vital.

Borrowing the idea from Moor Park, an early morning briefing was a very early initiative where any specific concerns about pupils might be raised. A weekly pastoral meeting was introduced, which avoided all routine, operational matters focussing entirely on individual children raised by teachers or Heads of Section. Today there are many more Management Information Systems, but back then, a spreadsheet with access for all – to submit entries and to check – was set up. There were of course the cynics, the doubters. Would a lighter touch, more focus on pastoral care, negatively affect performance? Would the school lose its dynamism and results deteriorate as a consequence?

Time proved otherwise. Supported people, in school or the workplace, are generally more fulfilled and happier, with better performance resulting. A cheery greeting, a kindly word, asking after colleagues' welfare should be a matter of routine but are easily forgotten in a busy day. Seek out a member of staff you know is troubled by something (in or out of school); words of encouragement and the offer of help pay dividends. Notice, watch, observe and, above all, listen – to pupils and colleagues.

Some years later, the parents of a Year 8 leaver kindly wrote, 'The school strikes the right balance by being disciplined without being rigid; being nurturing without being indulgent; and being ambitious without stifling creativity, individuality or even eccentricity among the boys.' I particularly liked the mention of eccentricity – it underscores individuality.

One aspect of the school's culture required little change: the sporting life. As one might expect in a boys' school, sport played an important part. This was another reason why parents chose TNB, with some fathers living vicariously through their sons' sporting lives. There was of course a competitive hierarchy with A to F teams. It was genuinely sport for all, though the A and B teams tended to have more matches, with the A team competing at national level in most sports.

I recall a meeting with one mother who was furious her son had been demoted from the A to B team, suggesting he should have started in the B team to avoid the disappointment of the drop. She did not react well to my response saying that we couldn't have all boys starting in the B team. Another mother ranted at the coach when her son was substituted off the field, saying he couldn't have been the worst player in the team. Sport for all did not mean pleasing all. Competition can be tough but the boys need to understand that life is as much about winning as losing – learning how to do the former graciously, with humility, and the latter with good spirit, developing resilience.

From the very outset I was enormously proud of our sporting etiquette – both on and off the field of play. In football especially, the professional role models we see do not always set the best example with foul play, tantrums, arguing with the referee and excessive celebrations on scoring a goal. As part of their coaching regime, our boys would be instructed not to argue with the referee or dispute a decision, and on the rare occasion someone did there would be words afterwards. In the event of perceived unfairness or suspicion of a refereeing error, it would be discussed later, away from the opposing team, their coach or referee. In similar style, if we scored it would perhaps be a cheer, a pat on the back, then ready for the whistle to start again – no shirts over the head or histrionic dances. When playing at home the captain would be there to welcome the visiting team and coach, with the whole team expected to stay until the visitors had left.

At lunch one day a boy came up to me with evident excitement and pride, saying, 'Sir, I'm captain of the Mighty Ds this afternoon!' The team coaches or 'Match Managers' instilled a corporate pride in all their teams, whichever letter of the alphabet they represented. For those less inclined towards the team sports – though they all had to take part – some diversification was needed with what might be described as the more individual sports. Swimming, which combines both team and individual performance, was a traditional strength of the school. I was thrilled one year when our Under-11 team won the national English Schools' Swimming Association medley relay. There were, however, other opportunities to be explored through a widened after-school activity programme.

One of my first appointments had been a new Head of ICT, Mark, who was also a keen and experienced sailor.

He and I started at the same time and, meeting in the swimming pool in September, he introduced himself to me. I had clearly made a strong impression at interview. Sailing was to become a new activity and thanks to the generosity of one family whose sons were sailors, both competing at national level, the school took possession of a small fleet of training dinghies. The sailing club became one of the biggest and most popular activities very quickly – despite the long haul to Bewl Water in the summer and early autumn terms.

Once the club was firmly established, Mark then explored an annual summer cruise on a sail training yacht, crewed by professional youth training sailors. This was 'proper' yachting: boys with duties, taking the watch through the day and night, doing the domestics, surviving seasickness. Trips included sailing across the channel to France, Belgium and the Frisian Islands, and another along the south coast to the Scillies. These were genuine life-changing experiences for the boys – they returned bigger, older, more resilient. So many pursuits, sporting and otherwise, learning how to manage disappointment, were intended to build resilience in the boys preparing for a world where competition is never very far away: a core mission of the school and, I would suggest, education.

I could relate to the boys' experience. Having just completed my A Levels, I sailed on a thirty-three-foot yacht with a friend and his family. Our skipper was a Yachtmaster who in a previous existence had been a bodyguard to Margaret Thatcher. Irrelevant but interesting; we knew we were in safe hands. We sailed to the Frisian

Islands accompanied by Erskine Childers' spy novel, *The Riddle of the Sands*, which was set in the area. Crossing the Channel, I was sick as a dog.

Through careful scrutiny of charts and precise navigation, we put down the anchor at sea one lunchtime. The tide was ebbing and soon, sand appeared around us. Before we knew it we were stranded in what was in effect a very large puddle. We leapt over the side and played football on the sand, surrounded by the sea. It was a carefully calculated but nonetheless risky move as strong currents constantly shift the sands on the sea bed.

There had been a shooting activity at the school for many years: The New Beacon Rifle Club. This was run by a retired marine and police firearms officer – a delightful gentleman. Again, we competed at national level, on occasion winning the Prep Schools' Rifle Association Hammond Cup. Shortly before he retired, the shooting master slipped and fell on the forecourt of a petrol station, sustaining fractures in both legs. I was amused to see a notice on the boys' board in the corridor: 'Shooting is cancelled until further notice due to the shooting master having an unfortunate accident.'

Not so much solely sporting, an abstruse range of other activities sprung up. One colleague had an avid interest in aircraft – accompanied by an encyclopaedic knowledge of flying history. He started a modelling club (of the 'Airfix' variety) for Year 5 boys, which rapidly became oversubscribed. At the end of the day the boys would rush to the dining-room to unpack their models. Very quickly the air would be filled with the fumes of modelling glue – no longer toxic. Another colleague enjoyed fantasy fiction and established the rather niche Dungeons and Dragons club, while an external chess Grandmaster rapidly gained a loyal entourage. The willingness of staff to share their gifts and interests always impressed me, underlining the broad range of opportunity available to these lucky boys as well as the talent of the common room.

Reflections 27.11.20

One of the many things we missed last summer was cricket – a fine tradition of The New Beacon – with a 1st XI which had the potential to reach the final stages of national competition. Siegfried Sassoon and his brother, Hamo, are pictured in 1901 having won the Kent Prep Schools competition that year. The picture was reprised in 2018 with our U11 XI who had again won the Kent Summers Cup, having held that trophy for nine years and been in the final for the last twenty.

Those who follow cricket will have revelled in Zak Crawley's 267 for England in a test against Pakistan this summer. Zak made his first senior appearance for Kent aged 17, just four years after leaving The New Beacon for Tonbridge. His captain at Kent is Sam Billings who left The New Beacon in 2004 for Haileybury College. Sam is currently in South Africa in the England T20 and ODI squad.

November seems an odd time to celebrate cricket. The reason is that we are thrilled to be listed in the Top 50 Junior/Prep Schools nationally in The Cricketer magazine which is published today. We compete at national level in

> *many sports but there can be few (if any?) Prep Schools who have two international cricketers of such standing and promise. We also have a former pupil playing rugby for England – which will be a story for another time as the spotlight falls on cricket today.*
>
> *Some might say such achievements are to be expected in a boys' Prep School. I would have to disagree, believing it to be much more than that. Yes, there is plenty of sport for all but, as with all things at The New Beacon, there is high expectation – we like to do things well. The boys are coached in technique, they work hard, they are encouraged to learn from disappointment, they practise and improve, striving to be the best they can be in all things.*

Early in any Headship, governors will be asking for a business or development plan: what is the vision, what are the strategic goals and what resources, personnel or buildings are needed to achieve those goals? Breaks and playtimes are a vital part of the school day, especially in a boys' school – they need to keep moving and to burn off some energy. TNB was blessed with plenty of grassy spaces and sports fields but when the weather turned wetter the cleaning staff would come banging on my door, frustrated by the mud or cut grass that was traipsed into the buildings. An all-weather pitch would be the answer, also meeting the ambition of introducing hockey to the sporting curriculum. Many boys played at the local hockey club and they would most likely play at their Senior Schools. This was the first phase of development, with two more to follow. The boys were thrilled to meet Mike Tindall for the grand opening and some rugby training.

There was already a sports hall at The New Beacon. The school had been ahead of its time with facility development. The sports hall was, however, no longer fit for purpose – too small and too narrow for a school of that size. It was also used for bigger concerts though the audience at the far end was too distant from the performers. I had already identified what I felt to be a gap in TNB's provision, which was drama and performance. Music was a huge strength (another significant benefit of a boys' school) with choirs, orchestras and ensembles. A small theatre with a capacity of about 120 was used for more intimate concerts and plays. Ironically, it had been the original gym. Public speaking – children voluntarily getting up to speak in front of a large group – is an important part of pupils' personal development and should be regarded as 'the norm'. Plans began for The New Beacon Centre – deliberately not named 'The Sports Hall', striving to address the perception that a boys' school was primarily about sport and everyone within was sporty. It was to be a building with a multiplicity of ambitions and uses.

As with many suburban planning authorities, securing permissions would not be easy. This was green belt land and, to compound, an Area of Outstanding Natural Beauty. We wished to have a sports hall which doubled up as a performance space, acoustically designed, professionally planned theatrical equipment, wired for light and sound with tiered bleacher seating. Perhaps it's the boy in me but this last piece of equipment, which emerges electrically and retracts to the depth of about a metre, I thought was simply magical. In addition there would be changing rooms, a PC suite and a Mac suite. A room at the top running almost the depth of the building was to be called 'The Studio', with views over the playing fields, used for match teas, seminars, table tennis – you name it. Every school needs large indoor spaces.

This building had numerous iterations as the planners wished us to reduce the footprint. Our clever architect would then reconfigure the internal layout, trying not to compromise the purpose or vision. A further aim for the building was community use, as was also the case for the adjacent all-weather pitch that had already been installed. For what to me were very obvious child protection reasons, we needed a visitors' changing room which did not have access to the boys' sports kit and this was where the planners wished us to reduce the size. 'You don't need so much space for changing rooms,' we were told. I have never before or since heard of a government agency – albeit local government – compromise, even disregard, safeguarding regulations. Planning was finally, eventually secured and The New Beacon Centre came into existence. The test of any new school building is the period of time before someone says, 'How did we manage without?' It didn't take long.

The third phase of development was the swimming pool. Again, ahead of its time and rare for a school of its size, The New Beacon already had a pool. At fifteen metres, however, it did not provide the optimal length for training and national competition. A twenty-five-metre pool was needed. Furthermore, the pool was leaking – water and money – with the infrastructure and plant held together only by hope and the brilliant estate team. This project would be for my successor as there will always be tasks and ambitions which remain unfulfilled.

On leaving the school some years later, I reflected on another task left undone. The Pre-Prep classrooms were wrapped around a large space filled with natural light, rather unimaginatively named 'The Central Area'. Creativity and imagination should be everywhere in a school yet, somehow, this had remained overlooked.

Two other operational changes were needed – both delicate as there were human, personnel implications. Food is a sensitive matter to boys and parents. The cliché 'an army marches on its stomach' most definitely resonates in a boys' school. The days were long, busy and active – for boys and teachers alike. Sometimes challenged by healthy eating evangelists, my priority remained for the boys to have options that would fill them enough to sustain energy for the afternoon; for sports and activities. A Reception boy at his first lunchtime came into the dining-room to see the honours boards and was heard to say, 'Look, they've got menus!' Honours boards dating back to the turn of the nineteenth century would be a comprehensive menu indeed. There was choice, however, with the more fussy often choosing pasta or a baked potato and fillings.

Without doubt, young people's eating habits have become more sophisticated over the years. These boys were lucky to eat in some very smart restaurants, not just Nando's. The tradition of 'table service' with a member of staff sitting at the head of the table and dishing out the food is now a relative rarity, cafeteria service having taken over, providing enhanced menu choice. Table service was a fine tradition in its time but practicality must sometimes trump tradition. Manners, though, remained an important part of the boys' social education. Early one Friday evening, Lucy and I walked into a restaurant in Sevenoaks to find a pupil with about a dozen boys celebrating a birthday with his parents and friends. To my delight (and just a little embarrassment), they all stood up.

The kitchen practice, menus and approach to healthy eating, did need modernising and the chef manager, by his own admission, had taken things as far as he could. We looked to outsource using a catering management company. Their task was to update everything food-related, including the dining-room, where bright, smart new serveries were installed, providing an attractive contrast with the traditional feel of the room.

The key to a successful kitchen is without doubt the chef manager. That took some time to achieve, partly because there was often friction between the cooking and serving teams. It was helpful to delegate this important element of the school to external management – the catering company – and while there were a few staff departures, a more unified approach was gradually achieved. Finally, we appointed the right chef manager whose can-do approach and shared desire to see boys filling their bellies meant we could part company with the management company.

The other change related to the school second-hand shop. This was an invaluable service for parents – cost efficient (can't deny the high price of new uniform), conveniently on site, while raising money for the school. The shop had been managed for many years by a team of former parents. It was situated in the basement and a signal moment for change was when it was realised we had a health and safety concern. These redoubtable ladies ran an efficient operation – tolerating no truck from their parent customers – but they were increasingly of limited mobility.

Our annual assessment by a Health and Safety consultant recorded the risk that in the event of a fire it would be difficult for the shop ladies to exit quickly and safely. The diplomatic skills of Kofi Annan, the former Secretary General of the United Nations, were needed and a relatively amicable departure (or retirement) of this formidable team was ultimately achieved. They had managed the shop finances on their own for many years, using surplus to buy things for the school – for example, an all-weather cricket strip. When they handed over the finances, it transpired they were sitting on over £25,000. In working towards achieving that amicable departure, we collaborated on where the money might be spent. The chapel was agreed upon to be a long-term beneficiary: a new organ and bespoke TNB hymn books were purchased.

Reflections 25.9.20

'Manners Makyth Man' – the self-adopted motto of William of Wykeham and subsequently Winchester College which he founded in 1387.

Despite the arrival of rain this week, the smiles of

the boys emerging from their cars in the morning is testament to the pleasure of a return to school. What we may have previously taken for granted, we have now come to see in a different light: school, lessons, teachers; friends and companionship. Structure and routine are important for children – especially boys – who need to know where they stand. It has been interesting (sometimes amusing!) to see boys moving around the site to their various commitments: plenty of chat and laughter but perhaps not always the customary sense of purpose. They are 'out of practice' having been out of school for so long.

In similar vein, the morning greeting. 'Good morning, Horace!' In response, 'Hi!'

'Er, no...' The formal greeting deserves a formal response. As well as missing the structure of school life, I sense an important social skill has eroded through absence – a distinction between the formal and informal.

We are proud of what some people might consider old-fashioned values which we would rather call good, solid, traditional social behaviour: manners. A parent recently mentioned to me that friends have commented on their New Beacon boys' good manners – a joy to hear. With the older boys I have been talking about formality and informality: from dinner jacket to denim; forms of address and greeting (no longer the handshake); formal language and responding to invitations in kind. An important lesson in social learning is to behave in keeping with environment and culture.

Today. 'Good morning, Horace.'

'Hi... [processing pause...] I mean, good morning, Sir,' with a big smile. We're getting there!

Influencing, shaping children, changing human behaviour – a core element and challenge of a teacher's role. It's not just the academic learning, it is educating the whole child: body, mind and spirit.

FRANKIE

Of course it came by text. With even the most open, empathic, enlightened, listening parents, most children do not find it easy to communicate their deepest, innermost thoughts. They don't yet have the emotional vocabulary. They don't want to be judged. They don't want to get it wrong; they wish to please.

My oldest, Frankie, born in 1995 and baptised Francesca, had gorgeous, golden ringlets. When only four years of age, on holiday with a lengthy delay departing Orlando, Florida, she walked up and down the line of waiting passengers, entertaining them with chats and smiles. A happy, bright child.

The separation and divorce of parents is what psychologists refer to as 'an adverse childhood experience'. This was undoubtedly the case for my children – not helped by the significant geographical distance between their home and my place of work, Sevenoaks and Ludlow respectively, which limited contact, especially during term-time. Thanks to my brother and sister-in-law living in Tonbridge, we had a base where I could spend time with the children of a weekend and they with their cousins of similar age.

Approaching eight years old, Frankie was becoming what historically and in the early noughties might have been described as a 'tomboy'. She and her brother would play with toy cars for hours. 'Big Ted' and Pooh Bear were important figures; time and memory may have distorted but I can't recall any dolls. She wished to have similar clothing to her brother and when arriving at my own brother's house would explore her cousin's wardrobe. Photos of that time show the now slightly darkening, curly hair, t-shirts and shorts, baseball cap, football at the feet. She was a skilful, talented footballer and, much to my chagrin, chose to support Manchester United.

A clever girl, Frankie achieved a place at Tunbridge Wells Grammar School for Girls, proceeding towards what would become a fine array of GCSEs. Something, however, was not quite right. In the teenage years, the mercurial struggles of adolescence, her behaviour changed. Not unique, you might think. The long hair was lopped. There was a series of girlfriends, mainly met through the local hockey club, where she performed at a high level. Alcohol arrived on the scene and I recall a prone figure on the kitchen floor, paralysed by booze, the story retold with laughter many times in ensuing years. We felt this turbulence was in part due to her fragile relationship with her mother, since she had chosen to come and live with us aged sixteen – never mind the upheaval of divorce.

Sixth form proved to be a trial. After a promising start with good reports and grades there was a decline in academic performance – unlike her performance on the football field, where there was considerable success playing for the Grammar School team. And then, out of the blue, came the text – possibly the longest text I've ever received and certainly the most poignant.

Frankie had had an epiphany – though only after considerable research, reading and soul-searching. I no longer have the text but recall it being reasoned and articulate. Frankie had been born in the wrong body, gender assigned by biology, by societal norms, by us. The concept and reality of 'transgender' was only truly beginning to gain traction in the UK in the first decade of this century, certainly for my generation. He'd found an excellent book written by a young, transgender person in the USA telling his personal story. Frankie gave me a copy, which I read with fascination and with growing comprehension, recognising so much of Frankie in this young person's history. Central to the story, too, was the importance – the vital importance – of parental support. For us that had never been in question, but reading of others' experiences can reassuringly affirm our own judgment.

Clearly, Frankie was leagues ahead of me on this journey. In my fifties, arguably born into convention, it was something very new; unexplored, unfamiliar and unknown. We should never be afraid to let our children educate us. In one *Reflection* (22.1.21) I referred to the words of a Tanzanian child from a book published by Dorling Kindersley: 'The good thing about being a child is that there are lots of opportunities. Grown-ups have already chosen their futures – there are no more possibilities for them.' An age-old, fundamental question: do we truly, actively listen to our children?

On opening Frankie's text, reading, rereading it again and again, I recall sitting on the patio; numerous cigars, coffee or wine (I cannot recall the time of day); tears shed and then sharing it with Lucy. How difficult had been that journey, epiphany, revelation and text for Frankie? My text response was simple: we love you, unequivocally, without condition, and will support you.

In due course the rest of the children and then the wider family were informed. Frankie's cousins gave their unpremeditated, spontaneous wisdom of youth, the older saying it was brave; the younger, it was weird. Frankie found both amusing, as did we.

Text messages exchanged, the time came for a conversation. Again, Frankie was highly articulate and reasoned, explaining how he had continued to question his confusion, his own gender, his place in society. All the research had lent sense to his very being; a gradual understanding he had been born in the wrong body. While operating in entirely new territory, I never doubted he was correct in his conclusions. Time, reflection and processing affirmed this. Looking back at his behaviour as a young child – the chosen clothing, interests and pursuits – genuinely nothing stereotypical here, just a recognition, an acceptance of gender dysphoria.

Turning to pronouns, these were possibly more difficult than an acceptance of Frankie's reality. Words are so important. In an earlier paragraph, without warning, the 'she' has casually transitioned to 'he' without preface or preamble. I recall meeting his new girlfriend and, in conversation with them both, I carelessly referred to Frankie as 'she' – the habit of years. Immediately recognising my mistake, flushed with guilt and embarrassment, I took my leave. When I got downstairs I immediately texted a humble, sincere apology. He was familiar and comfortable with who he was and the girlfriend knew his story, but it does take a little longer for parents.

Today the LGBTQIA+ agenda is universally known and generally understood – though perhaps not as widely accepted. All our own children are familiar with and totally accepting of their friends, whatever their destiny, their sexual orientation, their gender identity. I was particularly proud of Frankie when he told me he had set up an online forum and support group for those who wished to enhance their knowledge or indeed their own understanding of themselves. Perhaps inevitably there were those who posted offensive comments but well over a thousand young people benefited from the community he created.

As an English teacher, however, I do have a personal challenge with the use of the pronoun 'they' for someone who chooses multiple identities; we are still talking about one, singular human being. The conundrum: grammar or identity? It remains a purely grammatical debate in our household.

Reflections 1.10.21

Last Friday I was privileged to hear the legendary rugby referee Nigel Owens speak at the IAPS Heads' conference.

Those of us who follow the wonderful game of rugby will know him well as a brilliant referee who seems to balance control and discipline on the pitch with humour and a lightness of touch. His quotes are many: 'I don't think we've met before but I'm the referee.' He commands respect on the pitch amongst thirty big, aggressive men. Impressive.

Some of you will know Owens' story, coming from a small Welsh mining village, having a fragmented education, working as a school caretaker and farmhand. He claims his only ambition was to be one of the experts on Antiques Roadshow. Perhaps best known of all, he came out as gay in 2017 – an especially courageous decision in his chosen career. He says such a move was only possible with the support of his parents and, especially, the WRU.

The New Beacon mission statement refers to 'acceptance' rather than 'tolerance'. To me, the latter word has negative connotations: 'We'll put up with this.' Acceptance says something rather different whether it is about a situation or a person: 'You are who you are; that's fine and we respect you for it.' Owens' fundamental message in his address to some 400 Prep School Heads was about acceptance and how he has been accepted for who he is.

As I wander the school, in and out of buildings or showing round visitors, I take pride and joy in our difference and diversity. We are truly multi-national and multi-cultural. We are all different shapes, sizes, talents, backgrounds, beliefs, opinions. Part of growing up is learning to respect individuality and difference – something we feel strongly about at The New Beacon and something we endeavour to inculcate in the children.

LEADERSHIP STYLE

A common question at interview for Headship interrogates 'leadership style'. The first time I was asked, with the slightest of hesitation, I remember using the word 'collaborative'. A little research and there are plenty of websites overflowing with management-speak. It is a good question, however, for it is essential to reflect on how we lead – or our self-perception of how we lead. I like to think my style was definitely not autocratic, probably not authoritarian, but with maturity and experience there was certainly a quiet authority. 'Paternalistic' comes closer but does have a rather patronising air about it. My original answer, collaborative, is not too far from what I hope to be the truth, and a 'coaching' style could also apply.

I will add my own term: enabling. Every common room is laden with talent and sometimes in unexpected directions – the examples of clubs and activities at The New Beacon, I think, illustrate the point. Prep Schools are eccentric, idiosyncratic – at least, the best ones are. We are fortunate in the independent sector of education to have some freedom, though necessarily bound by legislation, statutory regulation and inspection. Prep Schools more than most can define their own mission and are then measured against it; too much homogeneity stifles initiative and creativity. Allowing talented teachers the freedom to explore and even experiment, unleashing them, gives them the space to inspire their pupils.

In my early days at Moor Park I had given myself the label of 'the late Mr. Piercy.' Timekeeping and punctuality needed some work. The draws on a Head's time are many and wishing to be available to all, the open-door policy, has its drawbacks. In that desire to give others the full attention they deserve, the clock needs to be watched. This is where the PA, Personal Assistant, is invaluable. I notice now at larger schools the 'EA' title – Executive Assistant – has appeared, and it always amused me getting a letter from one Senior School on the south coast from the Head's Assistant PA (which I considered to be oxymoronic). A good PA is an invaluable asset, gently but firmly coaxing and managing the Head. Thankfully I had learnt to be more conscious of punctuality, managing meetings, by the time I reached The New Beacon and a helpful ploy with my PA was to have that warning phone call after half an hour – whether another appointment was imminent or not.

A delightful weekly commitment was teaching the Year 5 classes. It sometimes took inordinate priority over matters and meetings more customarily the remit of the Head. After Year 4 the boys moved to the main building, following a secondary style routine, moving from subject classroom to subject classroom, from teacher to teacher.

This was also the time when thinking about Senior School destinations began in some earnest; when the nine-year-olds' conceptual development, character, potential and suitability for a choice of Senior School became more apparent. It was also the year group when registrations for the next intended destination, independent or grammar, had to be completed. Remembering lessons of the past – missing important English lessons – seeing each Year 5 class for forty minutes a week was the perfect solution.

I termed my Year 5 classes 'Oral Comprehension', which, roughly translated, meant I read to them. To miss the occasional lesson would have only minor implications, which included disappointment on my part. The lessons were great fun, full of laughter.

My choice was Roald Dahl's autobiographies, *Boy* and *Going Solo*. *Boy* had a certain resonance for pupils and teacher, being a story of Dahl's Prep School days. I would relate and regale stories of my school days while the boys could imagine and empathise with the experiences of the many boys before them who would have sat in those very classrooms. In one story Dahl writes of the long walk to the Head's study knowing he is to get the cane. In the form of role play I did the same with the Year 5 classes, walking down the corridor from the far end of the building to the other and my study, seeking empathy, with the boys trying unsuccessfully to stifle their amusement. If you haven't had the cane you might not know the churn in the stomach, the sweaty palms, the fear and anticipation of imminent pain.

On leaving school Dahl eschews university, joining

the Shell Company, and is posted to East Africa. There is a lovely line where his mother asks him if he would like to go to either Oxford or Cambridge – as if today the choice is that easy. He wants neither, seeking adventure. *Going Solo* tells this story and his experiences as a pilot in the RAF in the Second World War. Again, a draw for me was tales of East Africa, while the boys relished some of the eccentric characters he meets and his experiences as a fighter pilot. The purpose of these lessons, however, was to get to know each and every boy, his character, his confidence, his academic potential. One can learn much about a child in a purely discursive lesson, questions arising from the text (asked by me or the boys) where we might touch on figurative language, etymology, languages, geography or history. Armed with this knowledge of the boys, meetings with parents about potential destinations post New Beacon were much better informed. Above all, about the place, around the school, I knew them all.

Reflections 23.2.23

Teaching Y5 is one of the highlights of my week. We read Boy then Going Solo by Roald Dahl which give rise to an enormous breadth of discussion. We may touch on science, geography, etymology, ethics – anything which arouses interest; wherever the text and their curiosity might take us. Quarter plusses abound, and very often for an interesting question rather than a perceptive answer.

You may have seen the media furore this week with the Puffin rewrite of some of Dahl's works. Salman Rushdie is no stranger to controversy: we cannot be

> expected to agree with his views – neither, I suspect, would he want us to as a powerful, admirable exponent of free speech. It is good to see him and other influential figures speaking out against the 'laundering' of Roald Dahl's writing.
>
> We cannot airbrush history and we should not airbrush literature. We can however consider context, history, contemporaneous writing; conceding the mistakes of the past thereby informing 21st-century society and the education of young people. Surely it is acceptable – educative – to acknowledge the wrongs of times gone by to reinforce the rights of a more enlightened world today?
>
> In Boy we talk about the brutality of school discipline; the use of the cane in the early 20th century – how inappropriate it was and how much more civilised we are today. The lessons of the past learnt. In Going Solo we talk about the ethics of war – in general terms (and impartially) as all are very conscious of the current conflict.
>
> The challenge for boys (and girls!) is to be directed to recognise – to understand – what is morally wrong; then to use their own judgment and courage in making the right decisions.

Since the mid-twentieth century, the 13+ Common Entrance Examination for entry to Senior Schools has been the bread and butter of Prep Schools. Taken in June of Year 8 for entry into the chosen school in September of Year 9, it had been felt for many years to be rather late in the day if a pupil does not meet the chosen school's threshold and another school has to be found in a very short space of time. This factor along with Senior Schools wishing to fill and confirm their admissions lists has led to the gradual introduction by many schools of pre-assessments taken in Year 6. Such assessments generally lead to a confirmed offer for Year 9 entry, a provisional offer (often with a further assessment in Year 7), or no place offered. As a result there has been a gradual demise of the traditional Common Entrance exam.

For donkey's years it would not be long at any IAPS (Prep School Heads') conference before a lengthy, sometimes heated debate began about CE. It has its advocates and detractors. Some feel it to be an exam sledgehammer inflicted too young while others believe it is a good academic discipline in preparation for national exams at sixteen. Personally, and as Head of a boys' school, I felt it did develop good work habits while also acknowledging it limited the opportunity for research, critical thinking and independent learning. My own school experience of CE was, however, mixed. In history I foolishly confused the kings Harold and Alfred, the latter of course playing no part in the Battle of Hastings. An important lesson was learnt young: read instructions and the question carefully. Think.

As with many schools we had to consider how we would adapt and develop our curriculum since CE as a qualifying exam was required by fewer and fewer schools. In response to this emerging change, I gave the challenge to the Heads of Department: what would they keep, change, remove or add to their Year 7/8 curriculum? For some, nervous of change, they wished to retain the status quo. For others it was an opportunity for some creative thinking. We looked at 'off the peg' solutions – when there is policy change in education, publishers are quick to produce new resources – none of which were felt suitable, in keeping with The New Beacon's aims or parental expectations. We believed our mission to be distinctive. We wanted a bespoke solution which gave the opportunity for more creative, critical thinking and research while developing independent study skills – all of which had historically been rather stifled due to the restrictions and pressure of CE.

The Heads of Department, indulging in (and most enjoying) their own critical thinking, brought forward their suggestions and we arrived at a solution that we felt threw out the bathwater while retaining the baby. Exams would continue, based on the CE syllabus, itself based on the National Curriculum. Though the final summer exam was no longer a qualifying exam, the marks were still sent to Senior Schools in a bid to sustain the boys' (and parents') motivation. A science practical exam was added. In Year 7 a history project and presentation were introduced and in Year 8, an English Speaking Board exam. Philosophy became a curriculum subject in Year 8 – and the boys loved it, having an adolescent penchant for argument.

Reflections 17.6.22

Exams: bane, benefit or both? For the foreseeable, learning, knowledge and thinking will be tested by exams. What is our [The New Beacon's] approach?

Leadership Style

Until just a few years ago, 13+ entry to independent senior schools was assessed by the Common Entrance exam taken in the June of Y8 before entry. Today, the assessment process begins in Y6. Much can change in a child's development between Y6 & Y8. Today's system can dictate against a young 11-year-old while the old system left little time to find an alternative school if the CE marks didn't reach the threshold.

Regardless of the CE history, exams will continue to be the bar to be cleared for entry to schools, 11+, university, accountancy, law et al. Y5 did their first exams last week. Our advice to these very young men is this: it is just the very first stage of a long journey, working under formal, timed conditions. Testing knowledge and learning, yes, but early steps to develop familiarisation with working under timed conditions in a silent, formal exam room.

I asked some of the boys in Y5-7 how they had fared: if they were pleased with their results and why; where they were disappointed and why. The post exam period of evaluation is as important as the test itself. No great surprises here and pleasing self-awareness. One boy had done well in French because he had taken time to revise the vocab and grammar. Another boy, Y5, recognised he had not done so well because his time management had gone awry, he didn't finish the English paper and missed out on the most expensive questions. Lessons learnt!

'The only source of knowledge is experience.'
Albert Einstein

Moving with the trend, the Independent Schools' Examination Board (ISEB) introduced the externally moderated IPQ (Independent Project Qualification) in response to the demise of CE. This would be a precursor to – and in the style of – the sixth form EPQ, with boys choosing a subject, researching it and presenting it using one of a range of media: podcast, film or animations. In the first trial year, we were delighted with the results and the boys had enjoyed the process, their study skills enhanced.

This was an exciting educational initiative but necessitating the change was something less positive: the earlier assessment or pre-assessment of boys in Year 6. If a school such as The New Beacon is sending many of its pupils to highly selective Senior Schools, its academic policy can be affected by those very schools' own admissions policies. Parents will often have their first-choice school and a back-up option. Some will have several back-ups, thus the Senior School admissions team has somehow to work out if they really are the first choice and who might realistically join in Year 9.

Experience showed that year in, year out, errors were made with entry assessments and boys' confidence damaged when no offer of a place was forthcoming. In the early days, as this system was adopted by increasing numbers of schools, I recall one boy who didn't make the cut for his first-choice school to discover some years later he had gone on to study medicine after sixth form. Children develop at different rates and many boys early in Year 6 are still very much little boys where there might well be potential yet unleashed. Maturity counts for much at this sensitive age: you cannot accelerate conceptual development, no matter the intensity of teaching – or, indeed, coaching and tutoring.

George Bernard Shaw put it well: 'What we want to see is the child in pursuit of knowledge and not knowledge in pursuit of the child.'

Reflections 7.10.22

Returning to last week's theme differentiating between achievement and attainment: we are very conscious of the tests which Y6 boys have to take – or endure.

The 11+ exam, the Kent Test, has been very early in the autumn term for many years – a harsh and abrupt ending to the summer holiday. Our 11+ pass rate over the last five years averages at 86% and as I write, we await this year's results. The candidates this time undertook the challenge with considerable, notable resilience.

In a change over recent years, many 13+ schools now pre-assess in Year 6. Three groups of boys have been to Tonbridge in recent weeks with one group remaining. It is pleasing to see them all return having enjoyed the experience. Tonbridge and many other schools employ the ISEB Common Pre-Test taken in the autumn of Y6 (which follows later this term) testing reasoning, English and maths.

These tests are about attainment: reaching a certain threshold. For some boys there will be achievement, while for others there may be disappointment. Our view is such critical tests are inflicted too young, not always accurately reflecting innate ability. Although tests are age standardised, some Y6 boys are still very little while others much more mature.

We use the expression 'you cannot accelerate conceptual development' and witness, year after year, boys finding their way to the right school for them – in time. They give a much better, more accurate showing of their ability and potential aged 13. And, if this particular cohort of Y8 boys is anything to go by, they are confident (but not arrogant) and very good company!

STORM CLOUDS

The independent sector of education is vulnerable to economic turbulence or recession, generally feeling the shockwaves some two to three years later. My arrival at The New Beacon coincided with the collapse of the bank Lehman Brothers and the ensuing banking and financial crisis. Many parents in West Kent work in the financial sector and all Prep Schools in the area waited with some concern, anticipating parents with financial difficulties and pupil withdrawals. Oddly, for us the reverse was the reality and pupil numbers grew at TNB.

The same could not be said some years later when the word Brexit elbowed its way into our vocabularies and a referendum loomed. Economists and bankers do not like uncertainty; even more damaging is protracted uncertainty, which is what the heated political debate and impending Brexit vote brought to the UK. I remember it well as we had a huge school concert held in the Pamoja Hall at Sevenoaks School the night of the referendum – choirs, orchestras and flag-waving in the style of the

Proms. A straw poll of the audience suggested a clear majority for 'remain'.

The next day, when the result was announced, it felt like the country, local community and school were in shock. I felt, keenly, the subdued atmosphere in school. Over following months and years, the uncertainty and political mess continued. Families who had registered their boys for entry and were due to move into the area from London could not sell their homes. Those who had their boys in co-ed nurseries and Prep Schools kept them where they were, preferring stability, reluctant to change anything in their lives. Pupil numbers fell with fewer boys joining Reception, so we decided to open a Nursery for children to start the term they turned three years of age. Our market research indicated that parents wanted a co-ed nursery so girls were permitted at The New Beacon for the first time – though it was made absolutely clear Reception upwards would be staunch in remaining a boys' school. With hindsight we should probably have opened the nursery two years earlier, but once opened, and with good leadership, it became an important feeder into the school – an addition to the portfolio.

I tread with caution into the world of politics but something has to be said. Roughly 7% of the UK school population is educated in the independent sector, a statistic which has remained stable for many years. The pressures on state finances, an ageing population, the welfare state, NHS, schools and proliferating potholes can only increase, even without the volatility of recent years. In a stressed state education system, it is not uncommon in primary schools for two year groups to be combined with one teacher and an assistant. In secondary schools as well as primary schools, class sizes often exceed thirty. Some would argue it is the quality of teaching that matters most and more so than class size. My response would be it has to be both. The quality of teaching must be without question but the individual attention to each child in a class of fifteen to twenty rather than thirty-five is very obviously going to be better.

Across the independent sector there is real (and appropriate) concern about affordability, with fees rising at an alarming rate, overtaking inflation. Where once it was schools competing with the finest facilities, the sports hall or theatre, salaries and pension costs have become bigger threats to a school's finances. Many schools have a staff-pupil ratio of around 1:10 – salaries are the biggest cost with facility development, maintenance, operational costs and inflation to be considered. There is now the political threat of some form of taxation on school fees and it is likely to be the schools themselves that will be punished, incurring these additional costs. In turn at least some will be passed on to parents. Increasing unaffordability will result in children moving to the maintained sector, thereby adding further pressure to an already fragile, underfunded system.

What is the answer? My suggestion (in short and therefore somewhat simplistically) would be a government education voucher to the value of the annual cost to the state of a school place. Property values, postcodes and catchment areas already discriminate, pricing out and excluding some from schools they might have chosen – in some instances the flight to quality. Parents would be free to top up their education voucher at their chosen school. Not all independent schools have exorbitant fees. The Independent Schools Council (ISC) quotes the average day fee to be £3,000–£5,500 per term (2021), therefore only marginally more than the cost of a place at a maintained school of somewhere between £7,000 and £8,000 per annum. The suggestion made, I know it will never happen – too politically unpalatable and too much socio-political antipathy. A final, more emotive point, then enough said: is anyone criticised for choosing to join a private gym over the local authority leisure centre?

2020: COVID-19

Emails to Parents: 'Daily Update' March 2020 (abridged)

16th March
With the spread of Coronavirus, the rapidly changing situation and guidance, we will be sending a daily email regarding our response and any potential changes to school routine.

19th March
The inevitable announcement came yesterday evening and school will close tomorrow, Friday, at the usual times for the differing year groups. After School Club and Prep will continue to 5pm.

All teaching staff who are able to attend school will be here until Wednesday lunchtime. This gives us the opportunity to test our remote learning systems while also developing them, with staff taking part in training. We hope the intervening Easter holiday will allow further time to plan and deliver a comprehensive package of measures to apply from the official start of next term:

16th April. It is difficult to predict how events will unfold but we are anticipating boys may not return until at least after the summer half term and are planning accordingly.

20th March

We seem to be meeting ever higher hurdles – though challenge builds resilience. We hope one positive outcome of Covid-19 can be a greater global understanding for boys along with an awareness of their place in – or contribution to – the local community.

There will need to be considerable adjustment over the coming weeks. We recommend the benefit of routine for boys (especially on school days) along with plenty of fresh air and exercise. To help parents: these are the school's instructions and we expect the boys to follow them without a nag – to meet our high standards and expectations.

23rd March

Our new remote, distance world began today!

The whole of the UK went online this morning: remote learning and remote working. Zoom was also used for a choir practice. With both platforms, lagging and logging on difficulties were experienced due to traffic and bandwidth. Reloading the browser window sometimes helps. With OneNote there can sometimes be a delay before something appears on the screen.

It is worth noting that you can only access one account per device at a time: you will need to log out/in for each child.

We are all learning. My thanks to boys, staff and parents for their patience and flexibility.

Email Etiquette

We very much value good manners at The New Beacon – always a matter of pride when visitors compliment our boys. Email is a new vehicle for the boys so we thought some advice on communication etiquette may be needed. We accept that all instruction and response will be age appropriate!

Greeting. 'Dear Mr./Mrs./Miss...' for an opening email of the day; or 'Good Morning Mrs. ...'. Subsequent emails during the day need not have such a formal greeting!

Ending the email properly and politely. Not necessarily 'yours sincerely' but perhaps 'thank you for your help' or 'I look forward to hearing from you...'

Generally: avoidance of informal language, text 'language' and abbreviation.

24th March

The earth rotates on its own axis approximately every 24 hours. It appears we are in a similar pattern but lacking an axis.

Following the government announcement last night the school site is effectively shutting down from tomorrow, Wednesday. Our brilliant estate team will be managing site security and maintenance. There should be no need to access the school premises but in extreme circumstances please email admin@ which will continue to be monitored. Telephone messages will not be collected.

Just when you think you have a grasp of things, along comes a pandemic. The proposed mantra for a Prep School Head is 'expect the unexpected'. Surprises are rarely of the pleasant variety but with over twenty years of experience this was a complete unknown: the country and schools shutting down with just a moment's notice. Everyone will recall their own personal and family perspective but for the school community it felt like a bereavement. I recall one family collecting their son's belongings when schools were ordered to close on 20th March, the father saying he believed that would be the end of the academic year, without a full return before September. It seemed outrageous at the time but turned out to be not so far from the truth. This was the parent of a Year 8 boy and it was that group which would miss out on the wonderful, final Prep School term.

One aspect of the school's development requiring further investment was ICT. It was fortunate and timely that we had just taken delivery of twenty laptops, which, originally intended for senior pupil use, were rapidly distributed amongst staff who did not have their own personal IT equipment having both camera and microphone. Overnight we had to transform, magically, from a real school to a virtual one. The only thing in our favour was a few days before the end of term to construct and finalise a virtual learning programme we could trial and would have to roll out in full at the start of the summer term. It was in that short period our approach had to be defined.

We had a strong school community, now suddenly dispersed, having the potential to become fragmented. We were concerned for families, many with more than one very young child, isolated at home, parents trying to work virtually. It was vital, we felt, for us to support these families while doing our utmost to sustain the boys' education and schooling. Above all, we had to do everything in our power to sustain the boys' personal, social development; their friendships, peer groups and relationships.

We started with the now ubiquitous 'Zoom'. This remained our chosen virtual vehicle throughout these troubled times, primarily for ease of use but also because multiple faces were seen on screen simultaneously. Classroom management could continue virtually and it was important for teachers to see their boys' faces in an effort to gauge their attention, participation and, indeed, their wellbeing.

The day would start with a live form period, the class teacher being the central pastoral carer, with the register taken. Any absences had to be reported to the Head of Section. Repeated absences became not just an academic but also a pastoral concern and the parents would be contacted. Uniform was not required to be worn (though some did) but appropriate classroom attire was stipulated for 'live' lessons – no pyjamas or baseball caps. Cameras had to be switched on. We encouraged boys and their parents to create a dedicated workspace – their classroom. I would sometimes sneak into these morning sessions, which were often joyful, the boys happy to be together, taking my hat off to the inspiring and caring teacher.

We asked teachers to try to deliver one or two live lessons a day. Initially some were, unsurprisingly, completely out of their comfort zone in this strange, virtual world, but confidence grew with practice – as did their IT skills and capability. They were also very aware that parents were now in their classrooms. The most proficient were soon using the Zoom breakout rooms for boys to work in small groups – 'popping in' occasionally to keep them on task. The rest of the day was also timetabled. We sustained academic rigour as best we could, chasing inadequate or incomplete work or work not done. One kind Reception parent emailed to say his son had learnt how to read thanks to the online provision and encouragement of his teachers.

Our Head of Junior Sport would provide a daily challenge, from 'keepy-uppies' to a home-made bleep test. His pre-recorded tasks gave boys physical activities and challenges but also lightened the day, often to some hilarity as the boys sent in their own recordings. The art department provided artistic challenges, for example, asking boys to create 3D work in their gardens. The Head of Modern Languages recorded cake-baking in French, asking boys to do the same – and they did. The music department created virtual choirs, informal concerts continued and the Year 6 play still took place thanks to some masterful digital stitching.

We wished the boys to remain connected with their school. For some assemblies I would be walking the grounds or the playing fields, phone in hand, on Zoom. In their isolation we felt the community needed to see the familiarity of their usual surroundings. Their school was still there and they would return. I even took prospective parents on a tour in the same way. In the early days of trying to master these virtual communications, one sunny morning, I set off out of the front door to begin my wanderings, boys already connected, when I lost the signal – only to discover I had forgotten my swipe card and was locked out of the building. Rushing round to the back door and returning to the study desktop, we began again.

There were some very funny moments. One smart Year 8 boy recorded himself at his desk, put it on a loop and absented himself. His parents were informed but it was all taken with a lightness of spirit, recognising his ingenuity and knowing his sense of fun – punishment is not always the answer. Boys quickly learnt how to take control of the screen, much to the amusement of the class – or irritation of the teacher.

We gained an insight into homes and families – their houses were our boys' classrooms. Pyjama-clad dads would pass behind the camera. Cats and dogs would appear on screen. It was the new age of the home office and in the background could occasionally be heard parents on work calls conducting their business, the pressure they were experiencing felt through the ether.

There were also powerful, poignant, collective moments. Whole school assemblies and chapel services could be attended by all: boys, parents, extended family, wherever they might be in the world. Already an international community, we were now broadcasting globally. Some parents kindly emailed to say how much joy we had brought to their relatives in their home countries, who were feeling more isolated than ever from their families. The parents' association annual quiz was a popular event. Lucy and I decided to do it virtually one Saturday evening, parents afterwards comparing us to a couple off the live TV review programme, *Gogglebox*. With children participating it was a true family, community event and very well received.

The very first lockdown chapel service I remember for its emotion and novelty. The word novelty is more often associated with an exciting new experience; this one was novel in a topsy-turvy way and very emotional. The chapel was empty with the exception of Lucy at the organ and me at the lectern. There was some gentle organ playing before I spoke at my mobile phone, which was resting on a music stand just in front of me, live on Zoom. I spoke of the city of Norwich, which I could regard as my UK home city and which, anecdotally, once boasted a church for every week of the year and a pub for every day of the year. At the heart of the assembly was the fourteenth-century anchoress, Julian of Norwich, with those wonderful words, full of hope:

'And all shall be well and
All manner of thing shall be well.'

In such dire circumstances, not knowing what the future might hold, we all had to cling on to hope. Very quickly I realised just how much one instinctively, subconsciously gauges the engagement of an audience in the room, feeling their response – if they are with you; jumping with the high jumper. Education is a human business. To have that human interaction virtual and dispersed was unnatural, looking up to see an empty chapel. Even at the best of times I am moved, hopelessly and helplessly, by school events, performances, plays, concerts and chapel services. My voice would crack and falter, tears pricking my eyes. This was to be a frequent occurrence in those lockdown days, seeing those boys' faces on the screen while feeling the power of everything we were trying to achieve; the lessons, the assemblies, the virtual performances.

We felt it was important, too, to look outwards, giving support to the local community where we were able. We had school resources, we had minibuses with drivers, and reached out to help. A local pharmacy had no drivers, all struck down with Covid. A few of us made a rota, delivering prescriptions to homes across the Sevenoaks area, morning and evening. A local IT business selling and refurbishing computers established 'Laptop Library'. Families could donate laptops, dropping them at the front door of the school. The team would 'clean' and then redistribute them to those who had no IT equipment, their children therefore not able to access any live learning from their primary schools. Laptop Library set up their workshop in our Design Technology Centre and parents donated some eighty laptops, which were then passed on either directly to families or via local primary schools.

Medical services were of course at full stretch. Covid assessment centres were being set up in the car parks of both Tonbridge and Sevenoaks Schools. Having contact with some local GPs who were associated with TNB, Lucy leapt into action in galvanising parents, collecting the resources they needed, looking for donations, which we requested through our school communications. People's generosity was outstanding – remarkable. Somehow they managed to source PPE, which was in short supply nationally. Oximeters were requested, as were digital thermometers; they all appeared, dropped at the school front door. Clocks, portable whiteboards, markers – the most diverse range of goods was gathered.

A local cleaning company had a large supply of PPE, anti-bacterial cleaner and non-latex gloves which they donated – enough to fill a minibus twice over. The Covid assessment centres were set up in double quick time. An ingenious New Beacon parent with an engineering background designed an easily-made protective plastic mask and in collaboration with the DT Department at Tonbridge School, a production line sprang into operation, making and distributing some two hundred masks a day.

Reflections 8.5.20

Achievement

At school and in education we talk a great deal about 'achievement' and I wonder if we really think about the meaning and implications of the word. The Oxford English Dictionary defines it as 'finishing or carrying out successfully'. The Encarta definition, 'something that someone has succeeded in doing, usually with effort'. The use of *'usually'* amuses me!

Achievement is individual: one boy's times tables is another boy's spelling test. Every day there are multiple achievements by every boy often without conscious recognition. Finishing a piece of work or a task does not, however, necessarily imply achievement. Is the work incomplete, correct only in part, rushed or poorly presented? A line I sometimes use in boys' reports is, *'first past the post with work is not necessarily the winner'*. The key word of course is *'successfully'*.

There have been significant achievements over recent weeks by boys, parents and teachers. Grappling with OneNote came in the early days. Zoom followed with live lessons and the use of breakout rooms (bringing the challenge of supervision). Completing, returning and marking work via the correct channels now seems to be under our collective belts. These in themselves are major accomplishments over just six short weeks and that is without considering the academic progress made. Some of the boys' work I have seen is enormously impressive – as has been the teaching – and they are learning to work more independently which must serve well in the future.

But what of combined, collective, community achievement? In recent weeks we have thrown out challenges to the boys: photography, natural sculpture, cards and letters, singing and rainbows, never mind the daily PE challenge. In our first Pre-Prep Junior School Celebration Assembly I made the mistake of unmuting everyone as they sang their hymn. Chaos!

Thus the prospect of putting together 150 volunteer voices for the school rendition of We'll Meet Again was daunting. Poignant and powerful, this piece effectively blends the sentiments of VE Day 75 and our present remote conditions. Alongside The New Beacon WW2 presentation, we listened, reflected on the end of the war in Europe and looked forward to meeting again.

The image of a rainbow signifies hope and has become a fitting symbol for the work of the NHS. The challenge was to use any material to create a rainbow. More than 200 boys contributed resulting in another powerful, emotive presentation accompanied by poetry and music performed and composed by boys. It made a moving end to our assembly this morning attended by boys, parents, teachers and governors – The New Beacon community.

'The whole is greater than the sum of its parts.'
Aristotle

Reflections 9.7.21

The end of the term and academic year. What remains to be said?

We have received many kind emails and a recurrent message is one of gratitude to The New Beacon team, some suggesting that the teachers' very determination to keep educating, providing and caring for the boys has been a life lesson in itself. Teachers as role models – the way things are meant to be.

My reflection this week is on my colleagues – in

whichever capacity but especially the teachers and TAs – whose work and commitment this year has been beyond compare. Extraordinary resilience, determination, dedication, professionalism and good humour have brought us through to the end of the year. Nimbly and abruptly moving from classroom to virtual, they have sustained the boys' academic progress always with sharp focus on pastoral care, mental health and personal development. Thank you.

I leave you with the words of Carl Jung.

> 'An understanding heart is everything in a teacher and cannot be esteemed highly enough. One looks back with appreciation to the good teachers, but with real gratitude to those that touched our human feeling. The curriculum is just so much raw material, but warmth is the vital element for the growing plant and for the soul of the child.'

Many words and paragraphs could be spent on the subject of Covid but it is still too painfully fresh in the memory to dwell for long. With hindsight, and indeed at the time we realised, we were really quite fortunate having things to do. We had the outside space and sports fields of the school where I would practise with my nine iron. The boarderless Housemaster did the same while keeping a safe distance on the other side of the field, his young children also benefiting from the space and playgrounds. We had a skeleton school staff looking after those boys whose parents were in key roles, they too enjoying being busy, and working with the boys, striving to reach some semblance of normality. We had the brilliant maintenance team looking after the school buildings and playing fields and we took it in turns to deliver prescriptions. Our four 'children' had all returned home – we had company and some precious family time. That said, with planning, delivery, communications and supporting colleagues, the working days were no shorter than in normal operational times.

When it all began with the first lockdown, the parent who spoke to me suggesting we would not be back until the autumn was not far wrong. Some boys were allowed back later in the summer term, though Covid testing, taking temperatures and keeping tabs on registers was a daily, burdensome but necessary, chore. We read of clever children who could fake a positive Covid result by dripping lemon juice on the swab. When the gradual unlocking began, those year groups and boys permitted to return were delighted to be back in school even though the programme was limited and days shortened.

Parents were very good at following our safety protocols, which generally exceeded those laid down by government. There were inevitably outbreaks, one of the saddest affecting Year 6, who had been permitted to return to school. On a sunny Friday afternoon in the shade of an oak tree next to the NBC, I had to tell them their residential adventure trip was cancelled – a number in the year group had tested positive for Covid. This was yet another deeply emotional moment, a sadness which lingered for days. I can still see their shocked faces, some bathed in tears and misery – especially the boy who was due to have his birthday party that weekend. Just as they began to believe their normality was returning, it was once again snatched away from them.

One of the toughest and most wretched decisions – possibly of my career – related to Year 8. As already written, the second half of the last summer term for Year 8 in a Prep School is very special. Over the years we had choreographed what we believed to be a brilliant leavers' schedule for them. After exams they would go on a residential trip, normally to Le Touquet in northern France. I remember surprising them one year, just turning up to see them getting off the coach. One boy saw me: 'Oh, hello, Sir!' he said, seemingly without batting an eyelid, no surprise evident, somehow expecting me to be there. I like to think it was because the school engendered in its pupils a readiness, a preparedness.

After the leavers' trip the Class of 2020 would put on a play in under two weeks – normally an irreverent take on another play or film. One might not expect variations on a theme of *Mamma Mia* or *The Sound of Music* in a boys' Prep School but there they were, tremendous and hilarious. Before casting any play, the group was asked if any would be happy playing a female part – there was never a shortage of volunteers. After the performances, the mood would subtly change, becoming more poignant, reflective and nostalgic, looking back at their years at TNB while also looking forward to future challenges at their next schools. The black-tie Leavers' Dinner was followed by their final school event the next day, the Leavers' Service – Prizegiving having been the previous weekend.

None of this was to happen in 2020 due to what had to be a pragmatic decision. My Chair of Governors at Moor Park, amongst all the good advice, had taught me to separate the emotion from the data when making a difficult decision. An emotional decision would have allowed the year group to pursue the familiar programme. The data, however, suggested these boys would not be able to keep the regulated, safe distance from each other; infection would spread not just within their groups but into their homes and beyond.

We could not put on a programme of visits for them in school or elsewhere; it would simply not have been safe and, as it was, we were only just clinging on with those who were in school. The Head of Year 8, however, put on a brilliant, innovative virtual programme for the boys, dividing the cohort into 'tribes' with activities involving anything from a creative variety of challenges to film-making and a virtual play. Keeping to government regulations, they were permitted to have their Leavers' Dinner in smaller groups in different homes, connecting via Zoom. The tribes could meet at one of their houses to undertake challenges and to record their activities, which was about the full extent of permissible, safe activity. Many parents were kind in their appreciation; sadly, some never forgave us.

So much was lost in that time: friends, family, home and work. We hope never to see the like of it again. In a considerable irony, however, I felt the school emerged stronger, where relationships and connections mattered more than ever, the ethos clear to all.

Reflections 11.9.20

The return to school – at last! I have been speaking with the older boys about the Roman god Janus, the god of change and transition, pictured looking both forwards and backwards. September is the educational January, our new year, and what a new year it is after such a long absence.

Looking back, we must find the positives of the last six months. Many boys have developed enhanced independent learning habits which will serve them well as they move through the school. In chapel, a member of Y7/8 said we have come to appreciate health workers, the NHS, even more. Parents may also have come to recognise the challenges of teaching! We have felt the absence of freedom – not least the ability to go on holiday without fear of infection or quarantine. I asked the boys where they hadn't gone this summer.

The joy of welcoming everyone back last week emphasised just how much children, parents and teachers had missed school. I think it has made us appreciate all the more our good fortune, never to be taken for granted, in being part of The New Beacon community. And this was my major point to the older boys: perhaps we have come to value even more the importance of human relationships, having been deprived for so long of friendship groups, family and even teachers. It is those relationships which I believe make this place so special – I have witnessed numerous engagements between teachers and boys in recent days which powerfully demonstrate the great strength of our school community.

Looking forward, I wish boys, parents and colleagues a very happy, successful year. It's good to be back!

FRANCE

Somewhere around 2011, we decided a refuge was needed – a place safely distant from Sevenoaks. Heads, teachers, clergy and GPs are easy prey when straying from the safety of their schools, churches and surgeries. From a high street shop to collecting a prescription; from pub to restaurant, we are all in the public eye with privacy jealously guarded. When dressed informally – no suit, no tie, in shorts and polo shirt – many a pupil has stopped in the aisle of a supermarket, silent and staring, open-mouthed, shocked that we can exist beyond the curtilage of school and grounds. In the early days at The New Beacon, not knowing the face of every pupil, I soon recognised the dangers of smiling at young boys in shops, gauging the possibility he might be one of my pupils and, if so, fearing he might feel he had been ignored.

In one such encounter, of a weekend, I found one of my pupils who had become separated from his father. We began roving the aisles to reunite them. The father did not seem particularly bothered or embarrassed but my reward was a big smile from the boy when I saw him on Monday. A boy who I had bumped into away from school would say when I next saw him in school, 'Sir, I saw you in town yesterday.' Enchanting. On another occasion, getting a hot chocolate for my son one chilly, rainy Sunday morning after hockey practice, we bumped into a parent who greeted us cheerily. He made polite conversation and then threw in the invasive, killer question, 'So, Mr. Piercy, what is the school's strategy?' I hastily made my excuses and we left.

Lucy had a previous career where she had travelled the world as a buyer for a boutique wine merchant. She had spent months in various regions of France with producers, even participating in the grape harvest. We share a love of France – and not just for the wine. The food, the landscape, the culture, the sense of space are all appealing. We had taken the children to stay in a delightful *gite* in the Dordogne; a swimming pool dive-bombed by hornets, sitting on the wall in the evening watching the distant lightning. Knowing the owner was seeking to sell, an idea was born: a home in France. When deliberating location and area, practicality intervened, realising we would only rarely make it as far south as the Dordogne. We settled on Pas de Calais – three hours door to door on a good day, Sevenoaks being close to the channel tunnel and ferry crossings. Once in France the charming, historic town of Montreuil-sur-Mer is a mere forty-five minutes distant, served by good roads with the additional benefit of a beautiful coastline and some lovely, nearby beaches. This was to be our target area.

The search began. There was no shortage of choice; from dilapidated farm buildings to chateaux. We quickly agreed on a characterful *longère* in a hamlet ten minutes from Montreuil and half an hour from the coast. For 'characterful', read estate agent speak – a little run down. It has to be said the purchase was driven by emotion rather than financial prudence, but it was to suit us at the time. The family selling was British, returning to the UK, giving us the added convenience of purchasing a fully furnished house, the homely taste to our liking.

A huge attraction was the garden and wooded grounds; a large lawn to the rear then down a small slope to a further, tree-lined field. The children would wander beyond our unsecured boundaries, exploring the shell of an unfinished, half-built house, which of course was immediately classified as haunted. This lower field, a bright blanket of snowdrops in the spring, became bonfire territory. Lucy was an acknowledged firebug, taking after her father, who was always determined to set a fire without artificial incendiary liquids or devices. There was an abundance of fallen tinder, twigs and branches to gather (the task for reluctant children), with fat logs creating a surround for sitting as the nights darkened, marshmallows at the ready – often melting into the fire before reaching anticipatory mouths.

The children all being relatively young at that stage, it made the perfect holiday home for us all. There was no mobile signal or WiFi for the first few years. Even then, and not so long ago, emails were not as all-pervading. The children didn't yet have their own mobile phones, and any access to their other devices necessitated Lucy driving to a field nearer Montreuil. Playing cards, board games, Lego, reading and conversation were the order of the day, with DVDs in the evening. Family and friends would come and stay with food, wine and laughter in abundance, sometimes being there to see in the new year. On the very dark nights, with minimal light pollution, we'd lie on our backs on the grass or the trampoline, seeing the Milky Way and watching for shooting stars.

Away from the house, the weekly market in Montreuil was popular – wood-oven-baked bread, cheeses, charcuterie – as was our favourite lunch venue, Brasserie Le Caveau. We would walk the ramparts – which had a lofty disregard for health and safety, not a barrier to be seen, the ironic absence of a British obsession not escaping us. En route to Le Touquet there were the fresh fish restaurants at Étaples, close to the huge, emotive military cemetery with its imposing Lutyens monument. Le Touquet was of great appeal with the never-ending, sandy beach when the tide was out. Aqualud, a water park right on the beachfront, was a favourite destination for the children though less popular with the adults for its noise and indoor chlorine assaulting the sinuses, remaining for days.

As the children grew older, however, other attractions rose up the ranks of teenage temptation. Social lives, friends, sports and school commitments trumped family time spent in sleepy northern France. All now equipped with mobile phones, social media platforms proliferating, we eventually gave in to WiFi, giving a little more appeal. Fellow Heads, friends from the Class of '98 – by now affectionately known as 'the OGs' (Old Gits) – would join me for a few rounds of golf immediately after the end of the summer terms, practising with our nine irons on the scrubby grass in the back garden. It was a truly restful, peaceful haven – an escape from the world of work.

Looking after an already ramshackle house remotely was a challenge. We were fortunate in securing the help of a local lady who would periodically check the property for us. More than once she contacted me with reports of a leak – from a seeping toilet cistern to a burst pipe in the roof, water flowing down the walls through the ceiling, thankfully rapidly securing the help of a known plumber. Being so rural there was no mains sewerage and the cesspit (in French, *fosse septique*), as we ultimately discovered, was simply one of those large, plastic, reinforced agricultural water containers – inevitably prone to problems and definitely non-compliant. When we later added another bathroom and (compliant) *fosse*, I recall the contractor knee-deep in what leaves little to the imagination. He seemed unbothered.

With the commitments of school and our growing children, the visits became fewer and shorter. The pandemic years and lockdowns made access even more challenging. Our concierge caretaker, Marie, would check the property periodically, sending an email update, but an old house, prone to damp, unoccupied, was far from ideal and something of a worry. The garden and woodland was a concern, too. One email from Marie reported a fallen tree blocking the path down to the lower field. On the genuine premise of checking our property, having completed all the Covid travel paperwork, my son and I braved the Channel tunnel. While our journey was entirely legitimate with regard to Covid restrictions, we were still apprehensive of bureaucratic French officials yet we met no obstacle and arrived at a very chilly, damp house. The garden had enjoyed its lengthy freedom with the grass waist-high in places.

The fallen tree, with a trunk of a foot diameter, had completely blocked the path. We set to work with the chainsaw and as I cut the smaller branches, Ed took the axe to cut the larger blocks into fire-sized logs. With hindsight – and perhaps at the time – there was a sense of purging the confinement and frustration of the previous months in an absolute frenzy of activity.

Just knowledge of the house was a comfort, simply knowing it was there, while also seeming at times something of a pipe dream. Weekends during term-time were busy with sports fixtures and necessary, needed, uninterrupted time in the office. Work encroached on school holidays, too, with family time and gatherings a natural priority. I would sometimes run away immediately after the end of term for a couple of nights in an effort to cleanse myself of what were always a frantic final few weeks; in the colder winter months, checking, cleaning, maintaining, keeping the spiders at bay, with the homely prospect of a log fire in the evenings. In one unwelcome discovery, mice had burrowed in the bedding, leaving generous souvenirs of their visits. In the warmer, growing months, I enjoyed the ride-on mower, valiantly trying to repel the relentlessly encroaching jungle, vicious six-foot French nettles lined up in staunch defence. Nonetheless, happy times; a joyful, magical place.

TONBRIDGE SCHOOL

A year before Covid struck the words 'toffee' and 'caramel' discreetly, surreptitiously, crept into The New Beacon's vocabulary, under cover, in deep disguise. 'Toffee' was the code name for Tonbridge School; 'caramel' was The New Beacon. There had always been a long, strong association between the schools, it being no great surprise that many boys proceeded from us to Tonbridge, both being very similar in practice and ethos. To state the obvious, both were aspirational boys' schools. For many years every September, some twenty boys would join Tonbridge, which had been affectionately known by some as a big New Beacon – or New Beacon a little Tonbridge.

With roughly one eighth of the Tonbridge population coming from us, I knew the school well and came to know it even better as my son and stepson joined, three years apart. When in Year 8, both had been in the last days of Common Entrance (CE) proper. In differing ways they found CE challenging, though I believe their learning habits and academic self-discipline did benefit in the longer term. At Tonbridge both also took advantage of the Learning Strategies Department – nicely named, avoiding the label and what some might see as the stigma of 'Learning Support'. My son is dyslexic and thus the support he received was something of a necessity; effective and appreciated nonetheless. My stepson, following some years later, chose of his own volition to seek the department's support to help him with study skills in the approach to A Levels. A measure of its openness and accessibility, this was a refreshing metamorphosis of such departments from the early days of my career, with an infinitely better, widespread understanding of the diversity of learning styles.

Although with very different intelligences and leanings both young men found the pace swift; the level of academic aspiration ambitious. A parent asked how my son was getting on at Tonbridge and I replied in a most un-Sevenoaks way, saying he was 'on report' (meaning having a timetable carried around from lesson to lesson for each teacher to report on effort and commitment). The parent was shocked; I was delighted. They had found him out and had implemented a plan to restore the work ethic, ultimately bringing an impressive set of GCSE results.

I have something of a problem with 'prizes for all' and the implied avoidance of competition. Life is not at all like that. While there must sometimes be disappointment (felt in the younger years especially), as they mature, young people are not fooled so easily. Praise and encouragement, yes, but not given gratuitously. This was very much in our focus with boys – or rather, parents – applying for schools which had competitive entry and were sometimes beyond their reach. There is nothing wrong with ambition, indeed it is to be encouraged, but it has to be realistic, achievable ambition. A parent whose son was unsuccessful in getting a place at their chosen Senior School was angry and in a difficult meeting said, 'We don't tolerate failure in our house.' Unrealistic and shocking. Poor children.

Reflections 10.9.21

In chapel last Friday I spoke to the senior boys on the subject of 'patience'. In a world where everything seems to be immediate (or at least that seems to be the expectation), available at the touch of a button or swipe of a screen, patience seems more virtuous.

The expression 'good things come to those who wait' has evolved from the original Victorian 'all things come to those who wait'. I'm not sure I entirely agree with the former phrase ('You can't always get what you want' – the Rolling Stones edition), and most certainly not the Victorian derivation. Do we really expect to get everything we desire? The emphasis on patience, I do, however, support.

I spoke of the innovator and inventor James Dyson who embraces the making of mistakes, so long as we reflect on the prior flaws in thinking and practice, finding better ways forward. Over 5,000 prototypes preceded Dyson's first production vacuum cleaner; they got better and better. He had (and still has) patience, determination and resilience. We aim to build resilience in boys who, on the whole, do not like to make mistakes. We encourage them

> *to have a go and, if unsuccessful, reflect on the reasons, aiming for better performance in the future.*
>
> *Good things are worth working for and waiting for. In a school which prides itself on high expectation and realistic, achievable ambition, we do anticipate disappointment. It is how we face those disappointments, using them as learning experiences and continuing to aim high: picking up, dusting off and moving on.*

> 'Ah, but a man's reach should exceed his grasp,
> Or what's heaven for?'
> *Robert Browning*

Language is important; words have shades of meaning. Carelessly used or unthinking, inaccurate impressions are created. In school we avoided the word 'failure', instead using the word 'disappointment'. I am a fourth-generation Everton supporter – something of which the boys were aware. They were kind about it; empathic, even sympathetic. I would be the subject of some humour on a Monday – in fact, quite a few Mondays – after Everton had, once again, disappointed. 'Good morning, Sir. Did you have a nice weekend?' Polite pause. 'How did Everton get on?' They knew the result full well. In the occasional assembly I would refer to Everton in this context, saying I understood what disappointment meant: realistic expectations, keeping the faith, remaining loyal, sticking with it, developing resilience.

The Latin phrase and Everton's motto, '*Nil satis nisi optimum*' ('nothing but the best is good enough') could quite easily be applied to TNB, as it is to many other schools and an Air Training Corps. I have often been asked how TNB achieved its level of academic success and would say good teaching, without doubt, but also using that expression: 'expect little of children, they will disappoint; expect much, they will surprise'. It was as simple as that. In work, play, music, sport, everything; above all, how they were with – or treated – each other. The use of the word 'treated', however, evokes in me images of doctors and patients, creosote and fences.

Returning to the word 'failure': it is terminal. This is not just woke, political correctness (where I think the pendulum has swung much too far), it is a belief that language and words chosen carefully can make a huge difference. Disappointment can be reflected upon and qualified: were my expectations unrealistic; did I not prepare properly; was the competition too great on the day; did I have a bad day at the office? Similarly, I prefer 'acceptance' rather than 'tolerance', which seems to suggest one would grudgingly put up with something or someone. There is a negative connotation, whereas acceptance has a much more positive feel. The parent's comment about not tolerating failure was therefore, to my mind, doubly damaging.

My sons were in different houses at Tonbridge, benefiting from the pastoral care that comes from a strong, collegiate house system, whether as dayboy or boarder. With approximately sixty in each house, a Housemaster and tutors, there was excellent pastoral care, attention to the individual; always keeping them in sight, there was nowhere to hide. I was proud they both rose to being Heads of House. Thereafter, however, their paths diverged, with the older playing the part of Hamlet in the Lower Sixth, proceeding to the Royal Welsh College of Music and Drama; the younger to Cardiff University to study medicine. Look at any Senior School's sixth form output, not just at the league tables and A Level or IB results, but at the destinations and courses – is the school finding a student's strength and talent?

With James Priory's arrival at Tonbridge in 2018, as with any new Head's appointment, there would be a review of strategy. Tonbridge governors had considered a number of strategic options over the years: interrogating the 'all boys' status of the school; the ratio of boarding to day pupils; academic initiatives; curriculum development; overseas, Tonbridge-branded projects; having and creating its own Prep School; transformational bursary support – widening access. James and I had much in common in terms of educational philosophy; he was also a governor at The New Beacon and we got on well. We would discuss the threats and opportunities for both schools.

One threat to us was also a threat to Tonbridge. The increasingly widespread use of pre-assessments for entry to selective Senior Schools had pros and cons. One of the cons was what might be called the 'bird in the hand' scenario – an unintended consequence. With the instability of Brexit and national economic fragility, a trend was emerging. If a family was offered a place for their son at a school starting at age eleven, Year 6, they would often accept it, sometimes over their 13+ first choice. The less attractive alternative was waiting for what might be their preferred option, in this case Tonbridge, at Year 9. If they had the uncertainty of a provisional place and the prospect of another, qualifying assessment in Year 7, they would be tempted to take the bird in the hand.

This emerging trend was taking away potentially good candidates for Tonbridge while, similarly, the threat to TNB (and other 13+ schools) was losing more boys at the end of Year 6. Kent is one of the remaining few Grammar School counties. There are obvious, persuasive reasons for taking up a Grammar School place if the boy passes the 11+ Kent Test, but traditionally, few boys left us for other independent schools at the end of Year 6. We were keen for The New Beacon to retain its long-standing, successful status as a 13+ school.

From the Tonbridge angle, theirs was the only Senior School in Kent and Surrey that had no 11+ entry point. With some boys coming from London Preps, many of which finished at the end of Year 6, this supply would, in all likelihood, dwindle. The original Prep School model going back to the early twentieth century was eight to thirteen years of age; the traditional Senior School model thirteen to eighteen. Both have gradually moved downwards, opening up to younger ages, with many Senior Schools creating or acquiring their own junior section. For those families with sons in 11+ schools, Tonbridge could and would recommend local 13+ Preps to prospective parents for Years 7 and 8. From a parent's point of view, however, they would have to be very much wedded to Tonbridge to choose this path and change schools for those transitionary two years – if indeed they had looked at Tonbridge in the first place.

A further real concern was the very large number of Prep Schools, locally, nationally and internationally, which fed boys to Tonbridge. If Tonbridge was to create its own Prep School – never mind the vast capital expenditure and diversion of human resource – they would, potentially, take boys from their feeder schools. Some might say that is the nature of competition but a Senior School is all the better for drawing from a wide range of schools especially where boarding is at the heart of the community. They wished to continue supporting the wider Prep sector for not entirely unselfish reasons.

James, as fellow Head and a governor, new to the school and area, had good reason to discuss strategy. The independent school marketplace was (and is) becoming increasingly competitive. Furthermore, external, economic and socio-political forces were unlikely to diminish, putting existential pressure on smaller Prep Schools. With my governors I was keen to find a strong, sustainable future for the school. James, along with his governors, was keen to sustain the strong, local supply of boys from TNB. We arrived at the conclusion that there was mutual benefit to an even closer relationship between the two schools. Thus began merger discussions and the toffee caramel terminology. 'Project Lighthouse' was born.

The board of governors of each school created their own working parties. A merger committee was formed with governors, the Heads and Bursars. Early meetings were in person but then Covid struck and we continued virtually from our scattered locations. While there was a clear, shared purpose, there was also lightness and levity as relationships developed. A former colleague once used the neat expression, 'We should take our work seriously but not with solemnity,' an approach I have always felt to be of value and, sometimes, transformative when the matter in hand is delicate.

I will not go into the technicalities of different merger approaches, suffice to say ours was a 'full' merger with the transfer of New Beacon assets to the legal entity, Tonbridge School. It was in fact more complex than appearing on first sight with The Judd Foundation and the Skinners' Company to fit into the mix. While we were to be one entity it was also important for us to retain independence – in reality and in perception. We did not wish any prospective parents to think we would be directing all boys to Tonbridge – and neither was it the intention. Having sent boys to some twenty-five schools in the five years prior we wished to continue doing so – for the intrinsic value of doing so, finding the right school for each individual boy, but also to attract more families. We wished to fill the school. Tonbridge meanwhile was increasing its efforts and funding to provide transformational bursaries, 'Junior Foundation Scholars', often at 100%+ fee remission, some of whom would join TNB. These were very bright boys who would add to TNB's quality – we all perform better when we're surrounded by talent.

A further benefit for Tonbridge was the opening up of a hitherto untapped source of good candidates. They could now look at those 11+ Prep Schools promoting us as a bridging point for entry to Tonbridge at Year 9: Senior School foundation years. Most boys from New Beacon would proceed to academically selective Senior Schools and for some years, our Heads of Department had liaised with their counterparts at Tonbridge to see what they were looking for in a boy in Year 9 – not just knowledge, of course, but skills and learning habits. These links were beneficial for all boys and not just those going to Tonbridge, adding to our academic credentials.

At a very early stage we involved the expert, independent communications team that Tonbridge had been using to update their branding. The lead on this was a former regional CEO for Saatchi & Saatchi. We could not ask for better as he had the ability to tease out the strengths of the school, the key points, expressing them beautifully and succinctly. The communications were essential bearing in mind the number of perspectives and audiences. Would our parents think we had 'sold out' and wished to push all boys in the direction of Tonbridge? Would Tonbridge parents think valuable resources – paid for with their fees – would be diverted? Would other, competitor Prep Schools think our boys had an advantage over their boys, parents choosing us over them thinking their boys would have a better chance of gaining entry? These questions and more were addressed in the letters (to the various different audiences) announcing the merge and in the FAQ on both schools' websites.

The launch was delayed not just once but twice. The pandemic, as it did with so many things, interrupted progress. In the background, with the extended period of time, communications were redrafted and refined, which was to be beneficial in the longer term. Significantly, and to reinforce the ideology of the merger, relationships grew stronger. It is perhaps common sense but worth emphasising the importance of the personal rapport and shared philosophies of those most centrally involved in a successful merger.

The second delay was media attention to the 'Everyone's Invited' agenda. It brought into the unwelcome limelight many prestigious independent Senior Schools, with, perhaps inevitably, sharper focus on boys' schools. Tonbridge did feature but by no means at the forefront of either the testimonies uploaded by individuals or the resulting media attention. Soma Sara is a genuine campaigner encouraging those who have been subjected to what has become known as 'rape culture' to tell their stories. Adolescents get things wrong. Their left brain's emotional development lags behind that of the logical right – in very simple terms. They are also learning what is socially acceptable, influenced by their domestic, social and educational contexts; friends, schools and universities. With differing rates of development some teenagers will learn quicker than others, in part determined by environmental factors – parents, home, peers and social media.

Soma Sara makes a valid point about our society: something needs to change and she has been instrumental in this process, saying that certain behaviours, misogyny and sexual abuse, are 'deeply ingrained in our culture' and not just a consequence of environmental influences.

Although she opposes 'cancel culture', such a movement as that which she pioneered is a platinum-plated gift for the media, which misses no opportunity to castigate the independent sector of education. With the media focus on independent schools, and particularly boys' schools, it was wise to delay.

Reflections 23.4.21

A lovely, sunny start to the summer term with small steps back to some form of normality. Laughter has again been filling the air at break and playtimes after what seems like a long absence.

I have been reminding the older boys this week about some of the key principles of The New Beacon, drawing on our Mission Statement. 'Respect underpins every strand of school life... respect for 'difference' regardless of background, culture, belief, opinion, ability or character.' With reference to every noun in that list we promote equality and diversity in a structured way through assemblies and through the CPSHE curriculum (Citizenship, Personal, Social & Health Education) but, above all, through our daily being and living.

A parental dilemma: how much and at what age do we expose our children to issues of equality, diversity and morality? Or should we shield and protect for as long as possible?

Recent events, heavily reported in the media, remind us of the vital role we play in schools (and as parents) in recognising that equality and diversity must be intrinsic values in any healthy society. The cultural movement and

> *uprising following the death of George Floyd saw some justice this week. In a boys' school particularly, the issues raised by 'Everyone's Invited' are disturbing, relevant and an important reminder of our responsibility to inculcate fundamental, respectful, decent human values in our children.*
>
> *I think especially of our boys who will soon be moving on to secondary education where they will encounter many influences and temptations. The values to which I refer, which are espoused in our Mission Statement, which we reinforce in every area of school life, will I hope give them the moral courage and resolve to stand up for what is right and good.*
>
> *Returning to the Mission Statement, each boy should be 'aiming to be the best he can be' – not just in his work or pursuits but in his values and contribution to community. The New Beacon expects.*

In late May 2021, we launched the merge of our two schools with a carefully constructed, choreographed series of events. The first was calling an extraordinary, early morning staff meeting for New Beacon staff. Similar meetings had happened periodically over the pandemic so there was no great anticipation of what was to be an earth-shattering announcement. It became clear later that, other than those directly involved, no-one had had an inkling of the merger talks; the considerable, lengthy, ongoing work carefully concealed behind the scenes. Many other schools have gone through a similar process but with leaks and dilute, inchoate communications. While the delay had helped with communications and coherence, the possibility of a leak had been a risk. This was in the end, in itself, a real achievement.

It was a bombshell moment for the staff – there were gasps of astonishment all round. The first concern was, unsurprisingly, their own security. A longer meeting was offered later in the day where more questions could be asked and when they would be reassured of the legal process of TUPE (Transfer of Undertakings, Protection of Employment), which ensures an employee's rights and conditions of service remain the same. It did not take long to recognise this merge was a process that would take The New Beacon into an exciting new era.

Very shortly after that early morning meeting, my PA pressed the 'send' button on the pre-prepared bank of emails with letters attached and with a link directing recipients to the FAQs on both schools' websites. Meanwhile, James Priory met with his staff and letters were sent to Tonbridge parents. Mergers, acquisitions, consortia and independent school groups are increasingly common – a process which I believe will continue and grow. Surprisingly no-one had seen this one coming and it is now held out as being one of the most strategic in the sector.

Parents were invited to a 'live' Q&A with the two Heads and asked to pre-submit questions. We were still in the pandemic days of limited contact and gatherings so the double act presentation with the two Heads was done in The New Beacon Centre (being 'home' territory for our parents) in front of cameras. My mind cast back to delivering chapel services to an empty chapel and I was far from familiar with being in front of cameras, or indeed comfortable. James, however, was poised and confident, more familiar with the camera. Feedback after the event was positive in response to the carefully scripted programme that addressed the bulk of the parents' questions. The one which raised my eyebrows highest asked why parents had not been consulted.

The dust gradually settled after the launch. It was especially important for parents to see business as usual. In meeting with those who were considering Senior Schools, I made a point of emphasising options other than Tonbridge, though in truth, many boys were indeed ideally suited to Tonbridge, as they had always been. I made personal contact with the Heads of those other schools to which we sent boys, wishing to sustain those relationships, saying we would continue to recommend them to parents if we felt it was a good fit for the boy.

Within school, colleagues continued working on the Year 7/8 curriculum: monitor, evaluate, review. The Heads of Department now did this in closer liaison with their counterparts at Tonbridge, who themselves were scrutinising their own 'Novi', Year 9 curriculum. Over the years, and for good reasons, the curriculum has had additions, going some way back to ICT in its various forms; Design Technology; Citizenship, Personal, Social, Health, Economic Education. They were also experiencing a greater diversity of academic preparation with their feeder Prep Schools taking different and varying paths in their Year 7 and 8 curricula: The Prep School Baccalaureate – some, like us, creating their own, bespoke programmes;

others adopting more project work. It is philosophically right to keep as broad a curriculum as possible but compromise had to be achieved somewhere.

As for the boys, new experiences began to emerge. The sailing activity linked with its Tonbridge partner club. We had former TNB pupils teaching sailing skills to our boys. Year 7 and 8 had inspiring half days in the Barton Science Centre with Tonbridge teachers. Tonbridge academic Heads of Department visited, liaising with their TNB counterparts and teaching some of the older boys. A former pupil ('Old Beaconian'), dyslexic, returned to give a brilliant talk to the boys about his dyslexia, how he had learnt to manage it, proceeding to become a prefect at Tonbridge and embarking on four A Levels. He talked with affection about how TNB staff had provided the foundations for these achievements while also being accepting of his charmingly mischievous character – he did get into a few scrapes. 'I turned it round,' he told me.

The main aim of the first year after the merge was to begin building relationships, looking for common ground and considering opportunities for future development. At strategic level, work and research would begin on addressing the 11+ challenge, which had been a primary motivation for the merge.

Letter from the Head to TNB Parents (abridged)

Further to the letter from the Chairman of Governors, I am delighted that we can now make public the news that The New Beacon will be merging with Tonbridge School at the start of the next academic year in September 2021.

Every year some 20 boys from The New Beacon are accepted by Tonbridge – a determinedly selective school – and we are confident that will continue, contributing to Tonbridge's outstanding academic and co-curricular performance.

Parents can, however, be reassured that we will continue to recommend and prepare boys for a wide range of senior schools. We have sent boys to 21 other schools in the last five years and enjoyed considerable success in the Kent Test at 11+. Working closely with individual families, together we choose the school which is best for each boy. This bespoke service will continue unchanged: we will remain the 13+ school of choice.

As you may know, Tonbridge School already shares its facilities and specialist teachers with us. This will expand, allowing our boys and families to enjoy and benefit from, for example, Tonbridge's Barton Science Centre, art, drama and design facilities, its sports coaches and expertise in higher education and careers.

In addition, I am delighted we shall be working together to develop further an intellectually creative academic curriculum to integrate Years 7 to 9, building on the curricular innovation already implemented over the last two years. This will encourage the boys' work habits, support them in preparing for and sitting exams and to get ready for their senior schools – not just academically but in terms of confidence and life skills. These benefits will, of course, apply to all boys, whichever their preferred senior school destination.

In recent years, our boys have benefited from the refurbishment of the Pre-Prep building, the addition of an all-weather pitch and, most recently, The New Beacon Centre. The Nursery has added a happy new dimension to the school. We look forward to continuing to develop our teaching and learning environment, our boarding, co-curricular and sporting facilities, to deliver an outstanding, broad educational experience for all our boys.

KNOWING THE TIME IS RIGHT

Alison Willcocks at Bedales had been a brilliant, kind, inspiring, encouraging mentor and boss when I first embarked on Headship. She had risen to Headship through internal appointment, having already been at Bedales for more than ten years. She was pioneering: one of the first female Heads of an independent Senior School; a campaigner for the appointment of women to senior positions in schools. She was also a woman of high principle, respected by her colleagues and revered by her pupils. Alison chose to retire early after seven years as Head. Although she had been unwell, she did so for many other reasons, one of which being an example to those in the profession who might be sitting out time, waiting to access their teachers' pension. Tragically, not so very long after retiring, Alison's cancer spread and she died just a few years later.

We have all seen and recognise that mould of colleague that Alison Willcocks was trying to influence. The reserved seat in the common room: 'Oh, you can't sit there, it belongs to Mr. Tiggywinkle!' warns the comradely colleague, protecting the newcomer. Teaching is tiring but there is nothing worse than a tired teacher waiting for retirement. Vigour and inspiration fade in the classroom, recognised by pupils and colleagues alike.

The same principle applies to Headship. As soon as things begin to feel 'managed' or even rather comfortable, it is time to move on. I felt the time was right at Moor Park and the same again at The New Beacon. We had come out of the pandemic with confidence – the school's reputation and the community, I believed, were never stronger in my time. The merge with Tonbridge was one of the biggest strategic steps in the school's history and, as far as it can be anticipated with a prevailing wind, the security and future assured. A number of senior colleagues were approaching retirement, and having – to my own surprise – turned sixty, it felt right for my successor to be the one to take the merge and collaboration forward, to develop a new team and to build the swimming pool.

It is a dynamic job, one in which the Head should always be looking for the next opportunity, development, innovation, to take the school to the forefront of education. On many days it is the best job in the world and undeniably a privilege to shape children's futures. James Dyson borrowed a brilliant, succinct expression from the witty, perceptive Malcolm Muggeridge: 'Only dead fish go with the river.' Running the engine at idle, treading water, is not enough; it will seep through an organisation, colleagues and pupils, especially in the mid-twenty-first century where nothing stands still for long. Teacher, Head

– or any job for that matter – that is the time to consider a move.

Reflections 22.4.22

A great day was had by all at The New Beacon golf day at Wildernesse – parents, friends, governors and OBs of varying ages. I had the pleasure of playing with Ed (OB), 16 years old, a handicap of 3. Sadly and by contrast my own golf was a feeble, pale, wayward comparison.

To be clear, it was not my shabby golf which led to today's parent email from the Chair of Governors announcing that I would be stepping down in 2023: the time and need for more practice? Change is often good when carefully planned and considered – instinct suggests the timescale is right for change. Having had the privilege of leading this wonderful place for the last fourteen years and following the merge with Tonbridge it feels like the right time.

We are fortunate in having a strong, supportive governing board which recognises the remarkable (dare I say precious, unique?) essence of The New Beacon. Odgers Berndtson have been engaged in the search for a new Head and they, too, recognise what we have is very special. A change of personnel will not mean a change of ethos.

I informed staff of these plans early this morning. Once the cheers had subsided I outlined the above, the rigour of the search, the lengthy timescale of the appointment process and the recognition of all involved that continuity and stability can coexist with change.

Knowing the Time is Right

> *2023 is some distance away, until which it will be very much business as usual. Thereafter, I very much hope to be promoting and supporting The Beacon albeit from some distance.*

Taking up Headship in 1998, much has changed in those twenty-five years. A sample of 1998: the first DVDs were released, including *Jumanji* with Robin Williams; Bill Clinton, US President, was impeached; the Good Friday Agreement was signed in Ireland; Prince Harry joined William at Eton; BBC Choice was launched – the first UK digital TV channel; Arsenal beat Everton 4-0 to secure the Premier League. Those were the days.

I think and feel the world has become much more competitive. I recall a recent Head's training or refresher course where the speaker brought up a slide bearing 'WIIFM' – 'What's in it for me?' I thought he was going to talk disparagingly about a society that had become more inward-looking, more preoccupied with self. He was indeed talking of a societal change but not with the concern I had expected. The surprise came when he seemed to be encouraging us to question and consider 'WIIFM'.

At Prizegiving (Speech Day), after twenty years of Headship, I spoke about the emergence, gradual but perceptible, of a sense of entitlement in society, something about which we have to be especially wary in the independent sector of education. I told the story of a very small boy who was doing sport on the playing field next to our house, the Head's house, owned and generously provided by the school. 'Is that where you live?' he asked,

I assumed with all innocence. 'Yes,' I said. He continued, 'Why does someone keep taking a lawnmower in and out?' I hesitated, nervous of a trick question, but replied, 'Because he's cutting the grass.' 'You're very lucky,' he went on to say, and I agreed, 'We're all lucky to be here, aren't we?'

Google was founded in 1998. It was the early days of the internet. The mobile phone was the preserve of the few, a luxury item with a mere fraction of today's capability – for better or for worse – and certainly not in the possession of many children. Instant messaging started to appear in the late 1990s, LinkedIn in 2003, Facebook a year later, Twitter in 2006, Instagram in 2010 – and the rest, as they say, is history. These revolutionary changes have had profound, immeasurable consequences for the youth of today.

It is possible, probable, many generations think theirs was the toughest, but I feel deeply for young people as we dig deeper into the twenty-first century. It seems children are having to get older at ever-younger ages, faced with matters for which their developing, maturing brains are not yet ready. At The New Beacon we had a brilliant Head of PSHE (Personal, Social, Health and Economic Education), meticulous in research, planning and very professional in his delivery of profoundly sensitive topics.

As I write there is scrutiny of the Department for Education's 'Relationships and Sex Education' curriculum, which all schools have to follow. We had a discussion about some of the content that the DfE dictated should be delivered to eight-year-olds – and will have been in many schools. Without giving detail, we felt some topics to be raised with specified age groups were inappropriate for such young minds. These matters would most likely confuse and probably worry the boys so we chose not to include them. While we may understand the DfE's motivation, some aspects were certainly not age appropriate – in my opinion and in that of many parents. Subsequently, a media furore ensued when parents complained about some of the topics raised with their very young children, justifiably in my opinion.

The subject of social media is not new to any of us; it is a concern for all parents and those who work with young people. Social media plays to the predatory. It has an immediacy, making it a danger for the impulsive, emotionally immature adolescent brain. It is peer pressure personified. It is full of misinformation. A positive, however, is over the course of time it teaches young people to use their discerning, critical-thinking brain. There will be few Heads who have not had a call from the Designated Safeguarding Lead from another school or, on occasion, from the police. A pupil has photographed, posted something or forwarded it, and in so doing, may well have committed a crime.

We carried out a mobile phone, social media, gaming survey of the older boys asking about their usage – anonymity respected. I was impressed by their openness and honesty. There is frequent emphatic, forceful advice and repetition given by the school, now a regulatory requirement. These young people are very aware of the risks of their online behaviour. Ask and they know. Making the right choices, however, is an entirely different matter due to impulsivity, peer pressure and the temptation of immediacy, which a click, a swipe, willingly provides. That legendary, wise old Head of Hogwarts, Dumbledore, puts it well: 'It is not our abilities which show what we truly are; it is our choices.'

Many declared their parents did not activate 'parental controls', monitor their children's online presence or keep their devices away from their bedrooms at night. We would send plenty of advisory information to parents and invite them to live talks from experts, even specialist police officers. In one session a parent asked of the expert, 'Can you come round to our house and sort this out?' While young people face many challenges in their online behaviour, so do we as parents, along with a significant slice of responsibility.

Reflections 11.12.20

In our final assembly of term I spoke to the boys about an old TV programme, Tomorrow's World, *which featured inventions and innovations. A quick search on YouTube and you can watch two extracts, one of the future office and another about the mobile phone – screened in 1969 and 1979 respectively.*

The point I was making to the boys related to change and the speed of change – particularly with regard to technology. It was also about prescience: could we have predicted what has happened over the last nine months? The truth is we cannot predict the future with any accuracy even when witnessing the exponential march of technology and Artificial Intelligence. While there may be some mythology about the percentage of jobs our children will do 'which have not yet been invented', there is some substance to this research (or rhetoric).

We may not know the jobs of the future but we can be confident about the attributes and characteristics our children will need: problem-solving skills, adaptability, flexibility and, above all, resilience. It is our job (teachers and parents) to prepare children for tomorrow's world and, as always, we must draw some positives from the turbulence of 2020. The last nine months have truly tested resilience. I complimented the boys yesterday on their ability to adapt – they have done so with such good spirit. The benefits will be long term.

Reflections 21.1.22

What a strange world we live in – a sometimes bewildering morass of information at one swipe or click. A quick search brings up some marvellous stories such as Pope Francis endorsing Donald Trump's election campaign, and in 2017 the Dow Jones news feed accidentally publishing a technology test document which announced that Google had bought Apple (which was very quickly taken down). Covid alone has generated an entire library of misinformation.

With caution, I turn to the ubiquitous Whatsapp, a fine instant communication tool yet one which can easily mislead. With no ill intent a message with opinion or gossip can be sent on impulse which, forwarded many times, soon becomes fact. The dangers of social media – via whichever platform.

> *Online Safety is now a statutory requirement to be taught in schools. As one might expect it has been a significant feature in a New Beacon education for many years with a range of knowledgeable, expert speakers for both boys and parents. Much of the curricular content amounts to judgment, discernment, discriminating between fact and fake – 'reality check' has entered the vocabulary of the 21st century.*
>
> *NASA is installing internet on the moon. At first glance, fake, unbelievable, yet a trawl of reputable, reliable news websites brings some credibility to the story. This discernment is a core element of the boys' education: research, critical thinking and reasoned judgment – encompassing their learning in its entirety, not just online. They will, inevitably, make mistakes on social media but the more advice we as teachers and parents can give them, the safer they will be – and so learning happens.*

A great many of the oldest, traditional 'Public Schools' were founded to educate the children of clerics, the military or the poor. An obvious irony, therefore, is these schools having become the preserve of the very wealthy and, increasingly for boarding schools, overseas students. Costs and therefore fee inflation are a concern to all in the sector, with more and more families priced out of the option of independent education. There are fewer battered old cars in the car park – more four-wheel drives, for some a status symbol as opposed to a practical form of transport. There are fewer parents from 'the professions' with affordability eroded over the years, and most particularly the last decade.

In contrast to what might be called 'the age of entitlement', running in parallel with the culture of 'WIIFM', we also have the politics of envy. Public and political antipathy has never been stronger, with politicians no doubt feeling it expedient, vote-catching, to remonstrate at the unfairness, the inequality of independent schools. George Orwell's *Animal Farm* springs to mind, oft-quoted but relevant here: the aspiration of equality will never be achieved for 'some animals are more equal than others'. I know of many families who will forsake the summer holiday, a better car, a new kitchen or bigger house, choosing instead to invest in their children's education in an independent school. Back to Dumbledore, it is a matter of choice, which families should be free to make without embarrassment, or political or social censure.

In a career spanning thirty-five years (plus the two gap years), I have worked in eight different schools. Three were proprietorial and two of which have since closed (I like to think having no connection or correlation with my employment). The third remains successful thanks mainly to the genuine philanthropy of the owning family but also down to good leadership and nimble strategic thinking. Once a traditional 13+ Prep, it now goes up to GCSE, seeing and meeting a clear niche in the locality with a very well regarded sixth form college nearby.

The other five were all charitable trusts, two of which already had Senior Schools attached, and now a third following The New Beacon's merge with Tonbridge. As

I write, these schools' charitable status is under political threat; either that or the introduction of VAT or some other form of taxation. The last five years have already seen increasing numbers of smaller schools either closing or being subsumed into larger consortia.

The alternative to proprietorial and charitable trust free-standing schools is the growing number of school groups. Some of these are also charities, though an increasing number are 'for profit' organisations. In all schools cost control is vital – as is the desire to restrain fee inflation. Some of these more commercial organisations are stripping back the provision: staff-pupil ratio, class sizes, co-curricular options, breadth of opportunity, sport and music. The positive in this may well be keeping fees lower but one must question the impact on provision and value added. I would often say to prospective parents that there were two key reasons for making the huge investment in school fees: the staff-pupil ratio, often around 1:10; and the breadth of choice and opportunity – educating the whole child, stimulating the whole brain.

Of course this is all written from the Prep School perspective. The ISC (Independent Schools Council) Census of 2023 shows the largest number of schools to be 'junior' – up to either eleven or thirteen. Of the roughly 1,300 member schools, half have fewer than 290 pupils and a quarter fewer than 155. These numbers comprise mainly Prep or Junior schools, where financial margins will be very tight. The implications for the Senior School sector are clear. The writing is on the wall. The 'pupil pipeline', the Prep Schools which feed them, has of course to be sustained. There are some financial efficiencies that can be achieved: purchasing, operational costs, finance, IT departments et al. And let us not forget the educational benefits arising from the sharing of expertise and ideas through collaboration or merger. I would be surprised if the ISC census in years to come does not show a steady reduction in the number of smaller schools and would expect the Heads and Governors of these schools to be looking outwards, seeking affiliation or merger.

It seems that the world has been in a state of churn for many years. The UK has withstood banking and financial crises. Whatever one's views about Brexit, it has happened and we will feel the still-emerging consequences for many years to come. The pandemic has changed working patterns and, for many parents, made them reassess their work-life balance.

The economic repercussions of these seismic changes have yet to be felt in full as we watch the governmental purse strings tighten. The independent sector of education has not just survived through socio-economic upheaval in the past; it has continued to thrive, metamorphosing when needed. It will need to be agile, nimble and innovative in the coming years. The words of Stephen Hawking (or was it Albert Einstein?) ring true for our pupils and for our schools:

'Intelligence is the ability to adapt to change.'

IN CONCLUSION

Three Headships, all different, each with its own challenges, learning along the way.

I would arrive at my desk at 7am every day: fifty minutes of thinking, planning the day, checking the diary – waking up – before the staff briefing. One morning I switched on my computer and a message flashed up: 'Fatal error'. I laughed aloud: was it a computer problem or an ethereal message about coming to work?

The motivation of the job has always been the children: that is the simple part, the best part. Are they happy; are they safe, physically and emotionally; are they stimulated; are they challenged? The adult context of Headship – or any leadership – is more complex. Some very successful lawyers and financiers have said to me in all sincerity that they could not do a Head's job; the audience, from teacher to parent, from toddler to grandparent, much too diverse.

There is no intention to patronise in the coming paragraphs. What follows are purely personal views, some principles I have adopted and abided by along the way and which, I believe, have sustained me. It is only with hindsight I realise they have also guided me.

CHOICES

Decisions, decisions, decisions. Every decision has a consequence – something we repeatedly tell the children. With maturity they generally gradually learn to anticipate the consequences. The ancient Roman dramatist and philosopher, Seneca, recognised the power of foresight: 'The man who has anticipated the coming of troubles takes away their power when they arrive.'

As Heads and leaders we have daily decisions, from the mundane, the routine, to those that will have more profound, long-lasting implications than may initially appear, affecting the lives of others. There is a temptation to want to be seen as a decisive leader, which may be easy with some decisions. Without a full grasp of context, however, there will likely be problems further down the road in matters of more tangled complexity. Influence and sometimes acceptance will be more effective than trying to control – which is not to say avoidance or side-stepping is the right solution either. In the words of Theodore Roosevelt, 'In any moment of decision the best thing you can do is the right thing, the next best is the wrong thing and the worst thing you can do is nothing.'

When we become parents we put on a backpack laden with guilt. It comes with the responsibility of parenthood. I say to those parents who come to me with a worry or a regret, so long as our decision was not impulsive and we have acted using all information at our disposal, it was indeed the right decision at that time. We cannot accurately anticipate how contextual and environmental matters might evolve – we are not soothsayers.

Reflections 10.6.22

Some years ago a Junior School boy came to the study to be awarded an E [a reward for excellence] for a fine piece of work. With his form teacher he entered with caution, slightly nervous in a part of the building which at that stage would have been unfamiliar.

To some it may be a surprise that the vast majority of matters which necessitate a visit to the study are for positive, rewarding, congratulatory reasons. This was just such an occasion. As praise was lavished on the very young man, confidence quickly grew. Out of the blue came the unexpected question, 'What do you make in here?'

My immediate response was to say I try to make people happy but then came the more profound, somewhat esoteric answer: decisions. Decisions as varied as whether to cancel a fixture, a shirt sleeve order, an academic policy – or those rare occasions where there is a serious pastoral matter to consider.

Adults make many decisions daily, often without needing much forethought, using experience, lessons and learning from the past. For children it is different, where experience is limited and the brain still developing – the emotional brain more developed than the logical brain, sometimes leading to impulsivity.

COMMUNICATION

The pandemic, of all things, powerfully reinforced in me the fundamental importance of communication. Ironically, communication with parents has become easier with the use of the various virtual platforms. Reading body language, however, is a central part of any human encounter, enhancing an understanding of others' perspectives. I recall a meeting with a mother when at Moor Park. I listened and listened and listened, allowing her to vent her frustration. When I felt she had finished I said, with all sincerity, 'I'm sorry you feel like that. You're very angry, aren't you?' It was completely disarming. She had said her piece – much of which was emotion rather than data – which then allowed me to challenge some of her perceptions, providing context and perspective. We moved forward constructively. Ask a group of children what they understand of the word 'communication' and they will often say talking rather than listening. The same may of course be said of some adults.

Through the pandemic and lockdowns there were daily emails to parents as things changed rapidly around us and as we worked through the mire of government instruction. Much of the parental feedback during and following the pandemic praised the school's communications. Most schools have a weekly newsletter. Over the course of the pandemic, we brought together several weekly communications into one piece that had routine, operational information, news and reports of events, as well as boys' and classes' achievements.

At the top of this bulletin was the piece called

'Reflections' – on the week, the school, the world. It became especially poignant as we waded through the treacle of Covid but in time broadened out to cover a multiplicity of topics. It might reflect something happening in the wider world, cultural matters, a sporting achievement or any aspect of school life. Virtually all, however, reinforced in some way the ethos of the school, enrolling and involving parents in what we were trying to achieve for their boys. A wider point for me was the thinking; the reflection on anything and everything in school life.

'There is nothing either good or bad but thinking makes it so.' *Hamlet*, Act 2, Scene 2

Reflections 24.9.21

Following on from last week's theme which dwelt on encouraging boys to voice their ideas, thoughts and feelings, I spoke with the older boys on Monday about 'communication'.

For the young, the notion of communication might be that of speaking – voicing their own thinking – but the revelation is that listening is an equal part of communication. Boys are often in a hurry and their listening skills are not always what they might be. I have a theory (scientifically unproven) that boys go deaf when they put their hands up in class: they are focussed on their own ideas and imparting them rather than listening to what others might be saying!

While communication is about both speaking and listening, it is also about understanding. In the nervy atmosphere of an interview when a question is not understood or the answer not known there will be an impulsive temptation to make it up or waffle aimlessly. Absolutely the wrong course of action! While the received wisdom suggests a question should not be answered with another question, the context of an interview is different: a question to seek clarification or understanding is a wise move. It implies confidence.

> 'The biggest problem in communication is the illusion it has taken place.'
> *George Bernard Shaw*

COMMUNITY

In startling contrast to the isolation of the pandemic years, The New Beacon community grew stronger over those troubled times with a belief that we all belonged, a pervasive sense of identity and kinship. We were all in this together, doing our utmost to preserve – indeed strengthen – our combined mission: teachers, parents and boys.

In the early days at Moor Park it was not dissimilar. Those parents who loved the school, staying and remaining loyal, were forceful advocates as we emerged from difficult times with growing confidence. The staff, similarly, were unified in support and purpose. There's a lovely assembly where two pupils are put inside a hula hoop. One is told to get to one side of the room and the other, to reach the opposite side – on each side being an appealing, edible reward. Initially, in their enthusiasm, they are opposing forces, straining on the hoop, each trying to fulfil the individual mission. They soon work it out between them, going initially to one side then the other.

I have always been reticent about making my birthday known in school. It may seem odd not much liking the spotlight when in a role that is much in the public eye but that has always been the case. I had hoped my sixtieth birthday would escape and pass by quietly. It was not to be. I am convinced my wife was the culprit, having tipped off the Chair of the Parents' Association, for in the car park at drop-off, everyone, but everyone, children and adults, greeted me, 'Happy Birthday, Mr. Piercy.' Tiny boys clambered out of cars presenting their home-made cards and even the odd chocolate. It was deeply, deeply moving.

Reflections 13.11.20

On the evening of 11th November I wrote to my colleagues following our Remembrance service that morning – an extract follows. This solemn occasion remembering those who fell in the world wars (including some 115 Old Beaconians) was a treasured, rare, safely distanced opportunity for the school to join together and for families to Zoom in. Such things are all the more poignant in turbulent times.

On a special New Beacon day, three things occurred to me: our good fortune; the power of our community; how impressive are our boys (and girls in Nursery!).

'Dear All

In the last few days as parents have been dropping

off their smiling boys I have commented to some that we are the fortunate ones. While many are confined to their homes in 'Lockdown 2', we are able to come to work – to school – to enjoy community and companionship.

Today's Remembrance Ceremony embodied the power of our community. Some 350 children from boys and girls in Nursery not yet three years of age to young teenagers standing in solemn, respectful silence for more than twenty minutes – in itself an achievement. Staff from every area of the school joined the ceremony and we stood together to hear the prayers, Fin playing the trumpet, the choir singing and the musicians accompanying. We do these things well.

I was enormously proud today to be part of The New Beacon and I could tell that many of you felt the same. You all contribute to that powerful, palpable sense of community, creating an environment which is both stimulating and supportive and which provides such a fine education for the boys (and girls in Nursery!). With so much confusion and chaos around us we are indeed the fortunate ones.'

> 'If everyone is moving forward together then success takes care of itself.'
> *Henry Ford*

COMMITMENT

I recall a conversation with one retired, very long-serving, successful Head who suggested he had 'given too much'. I begged to differ. Teaching is a vocation, as is leading a school – an honour as well as a huge responsibility.

With the provisos of self-care and self-awareness, there is no escaping the commitment inherent in a Head's role. Returning to Churchill's assertion that Heads have more power invested in them than Prime Ministers, there is a danger here – especially on first appointment. Achieving the top position in a school does boost the ego but therein lies risk and, I would imagine, the same could be applied to any leadership role. I have not yet come across a training course entitled 'Experience'.

I wouldn't go so far as to say power corrupts, but it can alter perspective and judgment – give a feeling of invincibility. It has been an honour and privilege to lead three schools, to influence so many children and indeed colleagues but, as I would say to the recalcitrant boy repeatedly in trouble, 'no individual is bigger than the school', and that includes the Head. To be fallible is to be human and to be seen to be fallible (within reason) garners respect.

CODA

Rudyard Kipling is arguably no longer fashionable, perhaps because some would like to airbrush our colonial history. His writings were varied and various from short stories to poetry – sometimes controversial for their inferred empire-building undertones. Although highly successful in his own time, Kipling's life was tainted by sadness with the early loss of his daughter to pneumonia and his son, John, in the First World War, which inevitably influenced his writing. The New Beacon centenary book published in 2000 talks of members of the founding family, the Normans, cycling down to Bateman's in Burwash, the Kiplings' home, to have afternoon tea.

The poem *If* is a frequent poetic study for Prep School children and today possibly rather clichéd – undeservedly, in my opinion. Possibly written with his son in mind, it remains a wonderful litany of advice for anyone – and in this context, a Head.

It is Theodore Roosevelt's words, however, extracted from a speech made in Paris and given the title 'The Man in the Arena', that capture for me the essence of character required of a Head, in a bid to lead by example – colleagues and children alike. It is arguably a little grandiose, possibly melodramatic, to compare Headship with the leadership of a powerful nation, but I believe the principles still apply.

> *'It is not the critic who counts; not the man who points out how the strong man stumbles, or where the doer of deeds could have done them better. The credit belongs to the man who is actually in the arena, whose face is marred by dust and sweat and blood; who strives valiantly; who errs, who comes short again and again, because there is no effort without error and shortcoming; but who does actually strive to do the deeds; who knows great enthusiasms, the great devotions; who spends himself in worthy cause; who at the best knows in the end the triumph of high achievement and who at worst, if he fails, at least fails while daring greatly, so that his place shall never be with those cold and timid souls who*

neither know victory nor defeat. Shame on the man of cultivated taste who lets refinement to develop into fastidiousness that unfits him for doing the rough work of a workday world.'

Theodore Roosevelt, Paris, 1910

Reflections 22.3.23

The last fortnight has been completely overwhelming: emails, letters, notes, conversations, gatherings and gifts. I am truly humbled.

Once a believer in co-education, the conversion happened somewhere around 2004 in my previous Headship of Moor Park, Ludlow. We sent many boys to Shrewsbury School which, at the time, was boys only. I saw how boys thrived and achieved in that environment – tailored to the developing boy brain. In 2007 the Headship of The New Beacon was advertised. Governors looked kindly on my application and I started in September 2008. I have never looked back.

A rough calculation suggests 1000+ boys have been through the school since 2008 – all fortunate, too, to be part of The New Beacon community. Then we look at the multiples of siblings, parents, grandparents and extended family. The influence of the school spreads far and wide reminding us of the responsibility we carry as teachers.

It has been an enormous privilege to lead this wonderful school for the last fifteen years. My heartfelt thanks to everyone, boys (girls in Nursery!), colleagues and parents for your support and kindness.

BIBLIOGRAPHY & REFERENCES

Boy: Tales of Childhood. Roald Dahl. 1984, Penguin.
Cider with Rosie. Laurie Lee. 1959, Penguin.
The Go-Between. 1971, MGM-EMI.
Lord Cozens-Hardy. John Betjeman.
Peter Hain quote on Mo Mowlam. 2005, Wikipedia.
Blott on the Landscape. Tom Sharpe. 1975, Secker & Warburg.
Around the World in 80 Days. Michael Palin. 1989, BBC.
Harry Potter & The Chamber of Secrets. Albus Dumbledore. 2002, Warner Brothers.
Animal Farm. George Orwell. 1945, Secker & Warburg.
Independent Schools Council Annual Census 2023.

This book is printed on paper from sustainable sources managed under the Forest Stewardship Council (FSC) scheme.

It has been printed in the UK to reduce transportation miles and their impact upon the environment.

For every new title that Troubador publishes, we plant a tree to offset CO_2, partnering with the More Trees scheme.

For more about how Troubador offsets its environmental impact, see www.troubador.co.uk/sustainability-and-community